Second

Writing from Within 1

TEACHER'S MANUAL

**Arlen Gargagliano
& Curtis Kelly**

CAMBRIDGE UNIVERSITY PRESS
Cambridge, New York, Melbourne, Madrid, Cape Town,
Singapore, São Paulo, Delhi, Tokyo, Mexico City

Cambridge University Press
32 Avenue of the Americas, New York, NY 10013-2473, USA

www.cambridge.org
Information on this title: www.cambridge.org/9780521188319

First published 2012

Printed in Hong Kong, China, by Golden Cup Printing Company Limited

A catalog record for this publication is available from the British Library.

ISBN 978-0-521-18827-2 Student's Book
ISBN 978-0-521-18831-9 Teacher's Manual

Cambridge University Press has no responsibility for the persistence or
accuracy of URLs for external or third-party Internet Web sites referred to in
this publication, and does not guarantee that any content on such Web sites is,
or will remain, accurate or appropriate. Information regarding prices, travel
timetables, and other factual information given in this work are correct at
the time of first printing, but Cambridge University Press does not guarantee
the accuracy of such information thereafter.

Layout services: Page Designs International, Inc.

Contents

Plan of the book

	Writing assignment
Unit 1 *Who am I?*	▪ An introductory e-mail
Unit 2 *An important place*	▪ A paragraph about an important place and what happened there
Unit 3 *An ideal partner*	▪ A paragraph about an ideal partner
Unit 4 *My favorite photo*	▪ A paragraph about a favorite photo
Unit 5 *My seal*	▪ A paragraph about a personal seal
Unit 6 *Party time*	▪ A party announcement and a paragraph about a class party
Unit 7 *Thank-you note*	▪ A one-paragraph thank-you note
Unit 8 *Movie review*	▪ A two-paragraph movie review
Unit 9 *Friendship*	▪ Two paragraphs about a friend
Unit 10 *Superhero powers*	▪ Two paragraphs about a superhero power
Unit 11 *Advertisements*	▪ A two-paragraph advertisement
Unit 12 *Lessons learned*	▪ Two paragraphs about an action that you regret

Organizational focus	Editing focus	Just for fun assignment
■ Organizing an e-mail ■ Adding more information	■ Connecting sentences	■ Writing addresses and signatures
■ Setting the scene ■ Ending a personal story	■ Using prepositions	■ Making a guidebook
■ Listing points ■ Adding reasons	■ Combining sentences	■ Playing a matchmaking game
■ Giving background information ■ Writing a concluding sentence	■ Mixing past and present tense	■ Making a photo time line
■ Organizing information by location ■ Writing topic sentences	■ Using commas with *because*	■ Making a group flag
■ Writing plans and instructions	■ Using *so that* and *to*	■ Designing a poster for a party
■ Giving reasons ■ Using time markers	■ Using *before*, *while*, and *after*	■ Writing a thank-you card
■ Writing a movie summary ■ Writing a movie opinion	■ Using pronouns	■ Producing a movie
■ Writing supporting sentences	■ Combining sentences with *so*	■ Writing an article
■ Adding examples to a wish	■ Writing about wishes	■ Creating a comic book story
■ Writing attention getters ■ Using testimonials	■ Using persuasive language	■ Having a class market
■ Writing an explanation ■ Writing conclusions	■ Varying word choice	■ Making a card

Introduction

For a student who has never written more than a single sentence at a time, drafting a whole paragraph, even a short one, is a daunting challenge. Yet by writing even short texts, a whole new avenue for communication opens up. There are things students will write that they would never say, and writing offers them the potential to go deeply into their inner worlds. We, as authors, believe that all language learners, even low-level learners, possess a need to express themselves and share what is meaningful to them.

This book was written for such learners, especially those we call "3Ls": those low in ability, low in confidence, and low in motivation. Our goal was to create activities that not only allow them to succeed at writing English, but also allow them to express personal, meaningful, and sometimes fanciful facets of their lives. We have tried to create activities that pull our learners into writing rather than push them.

Writing from Within 1 covers a spectrum of educational objectives. Students are taught how to write sentences, generate and organize content, structure and sequence this content into paragraphs, review and edit what they have written, and, finally, respond to what others have written. We see writing as a balanced combination of language, expository, and self-revelation skills.

As in *Writing from Within 2*, the focus of each unit is a writing assignment. Some assignments are introspective: For example, learners are asked to reflect on something they are thankful for. Others are more conventional but task-based: Learners are asked to write movie reviews and advertisements. In this way, humanistic writing assignments are balanced with task-based writing assignments to provide a broad range of writing experiences. In addition, each unit ends with an optional expansion activity that gives learners the opportunity to apply their new skills to a different task.

The main task of each unit is the writing assignment. The first six parts of each unit are prewriting activities that have learners generate and organize information, learn basic language structures, and improve their expository skills, such as how to write topic and supporting sentences. Then comes the writing assignment. Following the writing assignment is an editing activity that helps learners enrich their writing by making stylistic choices, and then a feedback activity that gives learners the opportunity to respond to their classmates' writing. Each unit takes three to five hours of class time to complete, and although the syllabus is developmental, it is not necessary to do each unit in order.

The Teacher's Manual is designed to give specific ideas on using the Student's Book and tips for adapting it to suit your classroom. We suggest you take the time to familiarize yourself with the style and themes of the Student's Book before you begin teaching.

Writing is a skill. We tell our students that learning to write is like learning to play a musical instrument: The more they practice, the better they will be. *Writing from Within 1* is designed to demonstrate to learners that they have the knowledge and ability within to develop this skill. We hope they will enjoy this text, and we look forward to hearing your comments.

Arlen Gargagliano
Curtis Kelly

Guidelines for using *Writing from Within 1*

How should I use the Teacher's Manual?

The Teacher's Manual is designed to give you practical guidelines for teaching *Writing from Within 1*. Each unit in the Teacher's Manual is about six pages long. It is divided into three sections: (1) a short **Overview** that tells you what the students will do and learn, (2) a list of **Key points** – things to keep in mind – and (3) detailed **Instructions** for each part, which include answer keys and Optional Activities to provide further practice.

Whether you are a new or experienced teacher, we hope that this material will help guide the content of your classes. You know your students best; you should adapt the lessons based on the size, background, and length of your classes. Our advice is to follow the Teacher's Manual closely for the first few units until you feel comfortable with the book and then just use it when you need suggestions, answers, and additional activities.

What is the basic organization of a unit in the Student's Book?

Each unit has one main writing assignment. A unit is 10 pages long, and each page has one basic activity. Some pages can be shortened or skipped if time is limited.

Prewriting

Part 1: Brainstorming The writing topic is introduced, and writing ideas are generated.

Part 2: Analyzing a paragraph Students read a short paragraph for meaning and notice features of key sentence types. They are also given a chance to discuss a related topic in *Talk about it*. Here students discuss the topic of the unit and activate background knowledge.

Parts 3–5: Learning about organization, Working on content Students generate content for their paragraph and then are guided in organizing it.

Part 6: Analyzing a model Students analyze model paragraphs like the one they will create.

Writing

Part 7: Write! Students receive instructions for writing their paragraphs. Also, a journal writing option is included for additional practice.

Postwriting

Part 8: Editing Students focus on language and style points they can use to improve their writing.

Part 9: Giving feedback Students exchange paragraphs with other students for review and feedback.

Just for fun This optional writing activity builds on the students' newly gained skills in an entertaining way.

What is the purpose of peer feedback?

Peer feedback is not the same as peer correction. When students read their classmates' papers, they are exposed to meaningful models for their own writing and they develop their ability to analyze and evaluate writing. Writers get feedback from their peers to let them know how successfully they communicated their ideas. Since peer feedback puts the focus on the message rather than the performance, each writer is ensured a real audience. Peer feedback also makes the textbook easier to use in large classes, since it takes some of the burden of giving feedback off the teacher.

What are the *Just for fun* writing activities at the end of each unit?

The final part of each unit is an optional second writing assignment. It involves extending the language and writing skills learned in the unit to an enjoyable real-world task such as making a card, creating a movie plot, or designing a poster. Many involve speaking and group project work, and some of the activities also allow visually oriented students to add elements of graphic design, such as illustration and layout to their writing. Although some students do not like to draw, visual elements are an important part of written communication – they increase the ability of lower-level students to communicate messages they may have trouble expressing with just words.

How are grammar and vocabulary handled?

Grammar is not taught directly in this writing course. It is taught indirectly through exercises in which students are exposed to and asked to notice key grammatical forms, manipulate them, and then incorporate them into their writing. Vocabulary appropriate for the unit's main writing assignment is taught in the same way.

Can I skip certain units or parts?

The units gradually increase in difficulty, and features from one unit are recycled in subsequent units, but it is still possible to skip units or do them in a different order. If you do not have time in your course to complete all of the units, choose the ones your students will be most interested in.

Some of the one-page parts in a unit can be skipped if necessary. The *Key points* section of each unit in this Teacher's Manual indicates the minimum set of parts that must be completed in order to do the main writing assignment in Part 7.

How do I deal with mixed levels of students?

Deciding to put similar or mixed-level students together in a group depends on a number of factors, including learning styles, culture, and classroom dynamics. Experiment with grouping students in different ways.

Keep in mind that it is not necessary for every student to answer every question for learning to occur, and that the "compare answers with a partner" task at the end of many parts can help alleviate this problem. Pairing weaker students with stronger ones, in a sort of mentorship, can be effective in helping both learn.

A greater problem might exist when students finish an activity before the others and are left with nothing to do. Optional expansion activities in this Teacher's Manual and journal assignments are available to give such students additional challenges.

What is the purpose of the journal?

The journal writing task is an option for teachers who want their students to do additional writing or for use in classes where more fluent students finish the writing assignment sooner than the rest.

The exercises in the Student's Book guide students to write accurate sentences. The journal provides the opportunity for students to write more freely and develop writing fluency. It also allows both lower- and higher-level students to write at their own level.

Occasionally checking the journal is a way you can offer individual encouragement. We suggest you write short notes similar to the ones that students write to each other in Part 9. You can start with, "Dear _____, Thank you for telling me about _____," and then maybe share some of your own experiences, ask questions, or simply make brief comments. To encourage fluency, don't correct errors unless the students ask you to, and base grading on effort. Since students may write personal or sensitive information in their journals, make sure they know who will be reading them (just you? other students?). Do not let others read students' journals without their knowledge or permission.

How often should I give homework?

This depends entirely on how your class is scheduled and the type of students you are teaching. The book is set up so that most of the activities can be done as homework. We suggest that you give regular homework assignments so that students practice their writing skills outside as well as inside of class.

How should I evaluate students' writing?

This depends on your particular goals, as well as the grading standards set by your school. If making your students *feel successful* at writing is your main goal, then evaluate students according to completion, effort, and how other readers rate the writing. If *communicative competence* is your main goal, pay more attention to content, how well students organize their papers, and language use. If *correct English* is your goal, then spend more time assessing accuracy and have students revise their papers. Note that although many teachers set accuracy as the main goal and engage in extensive error correction, we do not necessarily recommend it.

In addition to writing comments on students' papers, we recommend that you meet with your students to discuss their writing, language goals, and ways they can improve.

You can choose whether to have your students revise their papers or not. If you do have them submit revisions, have them attach the original as well. You might ask them to keep a portfolio of all their work. You could give one grade for the original draft and another for the revision so that they have the opportunity to improve their grade. You could also give one grade for content and organization and another for language use. The most important point to consider in grading papers is that students need to be encouraged.

1 Who am I?

Overview

This first unit familiarizes students with the basic parts used in each unit in this book. Students are introduced to the writing process and learn to brainstorm, write a paragraph, and check and revise their work.

The first sections of the unit introduce students to the prewriting activities of brainstorming and organizing ideas. The central writing assignment of the unit, an e-mail letter of introduction, is presented in Part 7. The postwriting activities, Parts 8 and 9, include combining sentences with *and* and *but* and a peer feedback activity where students read and comment on their classmates' paragraphs. The *Just for fun* activity gives students practice writing their addresses and handwritten and e-mail signatures.

Key points

The activities in this unit help students learn more about their classmates, so they'll be comfortable working together throughout the course.

Take time to explain the purpose of each part as you go along so students will know how to handle similar parts in the following units.

Useful language for this unit includes the simple present tense to give general information.

Time can be reduced by assigning some parts as homework activities and using class time for checking the answers.

Sections can be skipped. A minimal set of sections might include Parts 1, 2, 3, 4, 6, and 7.

1 Brainstorming page 1

- On the board, draw a sample mind map grid (like the one on page 1, but without text).
- Tell students that "to brainstorm" means "to write new ideas quickly."
- Read the information box *What is brainstorming?* at the top of page 1.
- To give an example, say, *Let's brainstorm together.* Write *vacation* on the board. Ask, *What does the word* vacation *make you think of?* Write *vacation* in the center of the circle.

- Write a few examples on the board, such as *relaxation, beach, more sleep,* and *seeing friends.* Call on students for more examples and write them on the board.
- Tell students that the point of brainstorming is to collect a lot of ideas to work with. They can decide not to use some ideas later.

1

- Call on students to read the ideas from Hakim's brainstorming chart aloud.
- Explain vocabulary as necessary.

2

- Read the instructions for Step 2 aloud.
- Have students brainstorm about themselves. Set a time limit of five minutes.
- Ask students not to use a dictionary at this point to help them think in English instead of translating.
- Tell students they can fill in the blanks with any kind of information about themselves, not just the same information Hakim wrote.

3

- Read the instructions for Step 3 aloud.
- Have students introduce themselves to a classmate using the information they wrote in Step 2.

> **Later in this unit . . .** Call on a student to read this aloud.

> **Optional activity**
>
> **Party**
>
> Tell students to imagine they are at a party. Have students stand and walk around the room to introduce themselves and talk to as many classmates as possible. Set a time limit of 10 minutes. Then ask students what they learned about each other by calling on individuals.

2 Analyzing a paragraph page 2

Tell students they will read an example of a letter of introduction, and have them notice the language used.

1

- Read the instruction at the top of page 2.
- Have students read the paragraph individually.
- Call on students to read the paragraph aloud, sentence by sentence. Explain vocabulary as necessary.
- Point out that this paragraph was written by Hakim, whose brainstorming chart they read in Part 1.
- Read the instructions for la and the six topics under the pictures aloud. Explain vocabulary as necessary. Tell students that there is one sentence in the paragraph for each topic.
- Have students complete 1a individually.
- Read the instructions for lb aloud.
- Write sentence 2 from the paragraph in Step 1 on the board. Point out the comma between the two clauses and the period at the end.
- Have students complete lb individually.
- Ask students to raise their hands or nod at you when they have finished.

2

- Have students compare answers with a partner.
- Go over answers as a whole class.

> ### Answers
> 1. a. his job: 4
>   his interests: 6
>   his name: 1
>   his nationality and age: 2
>   where he lives: 3
>   his future plans: 5
>   b. I am a Korean man, and I am 20 years old.
>   c. I study English in / at a university.
>   d. Someday, I want to have a / (my own) family.

> **Talk about it.** Read this aloud and have students talk with their partners for about five minutes.

> ### Optional activity
> **Substitution game**
> Write the paragraph from page 2 on the board with the following words underlined:
>
>> My name is Hakim. I am a Saudi man, and I am 32 years old. I live in a small apartment in Rome. I work for an oil company. Someday I want to have my own business. Tennis is my favorite sport, but I like soccer, too.
>
> Students take turns reading the sentences aloud, substituting different words for the underlined ones.

3 Learning about organization page 3

- Tell students they will learn how to begin and end an e-mail letter of introduction.
- Spend a few minutes discussing what an e-mail is and polling students to see how many use e-mail.
- Read the information box *Organizing an e-mail about yourself* at the top of page 3.

1

- Read the instructions for Step 1 aloud.
- Tell students to look at Tomoko's e-mail. Read the e-mail aloud and point out how each part of her e-mail corresponds to the topics *name*, *age*, *nationality*, and *gender*.
- Have students complete a–c individually.
- Check answers by calling on some students to write their sentences on the board. While they are writing, walk around the classroom to check other students' sentences.

> ### Answers will vary. Possible answers:
> 1. a. My name is Min Ho.
>   b. I am 19 years old.
>   c. I am a Korean man.

2

- Read the instructions for Step 2 aloud.
- Call on a student to read the phrases in the Word Files aloud. Point out that greetings come at the beginning of a letter and closings come at the end, just before the writer's name.

- Point out that *Hello,* and *Hi there!* are informal greetings used between friends and family members.
- Have students complete Step 2 individually.
- You may want to take additional class time to correct errors on individual letters, or you can have students copy their letters onto a separate sheet of paper to turn in for correction.
- You may also have volunteers write their e-mail excerpts on the board. Go over them with the whole class.

Answers will vary. Possible answers:

Hello Jun Hee,

My name is Kazu. I am 20 years old.

I am a Japanese man.

Take care,

Kazu

Optional activity

Additional greetings and closings

Have students find some more greetings and closings. They can use their own knowledge, look in books or on the Internet, or ask native speakers. They should also find out whether the greetings and closings are formal or informal.

---

4 Working on content page 4

Tell students they will learn what topics to write about in a letter of introduction.

1

- Have a student read the top of page 4, including the topics.
- Read the instructions for Step 1 aloud.
- Read 1a aloud. Point out that the topic comes from the list at the top of page 4.
- Call on a student to read the example sentence aloud. Tell students to write sentences about themselves and their lives.
- Have students complete 1b–h individually. Walk around the classroom, helping students as necessary.
- Elicit responses from the class.

Answers will vary. Possible answers:

1. a. school: I go to a university.
   b. interests: I go snowboarding in my free time.
   c. future plans: I want to be an engineer.
   d. job: I don't have a job.
   e. where you live: I live outside Boston.
   f. friends: My best friend lives near me.
   g. likes and dislikes: I don't like hot weather.
   h. family: I live with my parents and my grandmother.

2

- Read the instructions for Step 2 aloud.
- Call on students to read their sentences aloud, or you can have students write their sentences on the board and then read them aloud. Encourage and correct as needed.

Optional activity

Who is it?

Have students write sentences about the topics in Step 1 on small pieces of paper and put them into a bag. Mix them up and have each student draw one out. Have students read the sentence aloud and guess who wrote it. Turn this into a game by having students stand up and ask questions to discover the writer (e.g., *Are you a junior college student?*).

---

5 Learning more about organization
page 5

- Tell students they will learn about how to add more information to the topics from Part 4.
- Read the information box *Adding more information* at the top of page 5.

1

- Read the instructions for Step 1 aloud.
- Have students complete 1a–c individually.
- Walk around the classroom, helping students as necessary.

2

- Read the instructions for Step 2 aloud.
- Call on students to read their sentences aloud or write them on the board. You may also have students read their sentences in groups and choose the most interesting answers to share with the rest of the class.

Answers will vary. Possible answers:

2. a. School: I go to a university. I will graduate in February.
    b. Friends: I have two best friends. Their names are Cintia and Sofia. They live in Brazil.
    c. Family: I live with my parents and my grandmother. She is 86 years old.
    d. Where I live: I live in a small town near Yokohama. It is famous for its beaches.

Optional activity

Matching follow-up information

Have students write their "sentences" and "more information" from Step 2 on separate slips of paper. Put students in groups of three and have them combine and shuffle their slips of paper. Have them exchange their set with another group. Students in each group work together to figure out which "more information" goes with which "sentence."

---

6 Analyzing a model   page 6

Tell students that as the main writing assignment for this unit, they will write an e-mail introducing themselves. They will use the information they brainstormed in previous sections.

1

- Read the instructions for Step 1 aloud.
- Have students read the letter individually.
- Call on students to read the letter aloud.
- Have students complete 1a–d individually. Walk around the classroom, helping students as necessary.

Answers

1. a. greeting: Dear Mr. and Mrs. Jones,
        closing: Sincerely, Tomoko
    b. I am a 24-year-old Japanese woman.
    c. where she lives
        her family
        her future plans
        her interests
        her school
    d. See you soon, Thank you, Best regards,

2

- Read the instruction for Step 2 aloud.
- Have students review in pairs. Call on pairs to review as a class.
- Go over answers as a whole class.

---

7 Write!   page 7

1

- Read the instructions for Step 1 aloud.
- Have students work individually to choose the recipient of their e-mail.

2

- Read the instructions for Step 2 aloud.
- Have students write their letter on lined paper or type it. Have them skip lines so that they can edit their letter more easily and you can correct it more easily.
- Have students complete their letter in class or at home.
- Students can also e-mail their letter to you and to classmates.
- Students who finish early should begin the journal assignment.

In your journal . . . If time permits, read the journal entry instructions aloud. Tell students they can answer one or both questions (see notes on page viii for more information on the journal). Have students complete the journal in class or at home.

---

8 Editing page 8

- Read the information box *Connecting sentences* at the top of page 8.
- Explain that *and* joins two ideas that are similar and that *but* joins two ideas that are contradictory or unexpected.

1

- Read the instructions for Step 1 aloud.
- Call on students to read the e-mail aloud, sentence by sentence. Explain vocabulary as necessary.
- Call on a student to read the example aloud. Point out the comma after *Korean* and how *but* is used to join the sentences.
- Have students complete 1a–e individually and then compare answers with a partner.
- Walk around the classroom, helping students as necessary.
- Check answers by calling on students to write the sentences on the board.

> ### Answers
> 1. a. I am a Mexican woman, but I live in the United States.
>   b. I have traveled a lot, but I have never been to Canada.
>   c. I love science, and I want to study biology in college.
>   d. In my free time, I like listening to music, and I like singing, too.
>   e. Please write back to me and tell me something about yourself.

2

- Read the instructions for Step 2 aloud.
- If students want to connect any sentences in their letter of introduction from Part 7 with *and* or *but*, give them time to revise their letters, or assign it as homework.
- Ask for volunteers to write their original sentences and their revisions on the board.

9 Giving feedback page 9

Tell students that they are going to read each other's e-mails of introduction, and that they will need a sheet of paper for Step 2.

1

- Read the instructions for Steps 1 and 1a–d aloud.
- Have students exchange letters with a partner.
- Have students complete 1a–d individually. Walk around the classroom, helping students as necessary.
- When they finish, tell students to exchange books and review their partner's answers. They can then go on to Step 2.

2

- Read the instructions for Step 2 aloud.
- Read or call on a student to read the example letter aloud. Point out the greeting, the closing, the sentence that says what the student liked, and the question.
- Have students write their letter to their partner individually.
- Walk around the classroom, helping students as necessary.

3

- Read the instructions for Step 3 aloud.
- Have students exchange their letters with their partner. Give them time to tell their partner the answer to the question in the letter.
- Have students revise their e-mails based on the comments they receive and other ideas they have. They can complete their revisions either in class or at home.
- Have students turn in their revised e-mails of introduction to you (see notes on page viii about evaluating student writing).

> ### Optional activity
> #### Who are we?
> Have students add a photo or drawing of themselves to their letters of introduction and display them around the classroom. Consider compiling them into a class newsletter or "yearbook" and distributing a copy to each student.

Just for fun page 10

Tell students they are going to write their addresses in English and practice signing their names and writing e-mail signatures.

1

- Read the instructions for Step 1 and the example addresses aloud.
- Point out that in English, information in an address is ordered from the most specific to the most general.
- Write your own home or school address on the board as an additional example.
- Have students write their own addresses individually. Walk around the classroom, helping students as necessary.
- Call on volunteers to write their addresses on the board.

2

- Read the instructions for Step 2 aloud.
- Have students sign their names. They may want to practice several times on a separate sheet of paper.
- Have volunteers sign their names on the board, or pass around a sheet of paper for each student to sign. When all students have signed, post it on the classroom wall.

3

- Read the instructions for Step 3 and the example e-mail signature aloud.
- Elicit from students the kind of information that is in the example e-mail signature.
- Have students write their e-mail signatures and compare with a partner or small group.

2 *An important place*

Overview

In this unit, students write a paragraph about a special place and event from their childhood. They learn to set the scene and write an ending for a personal story.

In the prewriting activities, students brainstorm and organize details about the place and event. They combine and organize their ideas to write their story in Part 7. Part 8 gives them additional practice using prepositional phrases to add details to their stories. The *Just for fun* activity allows visually oriented students to combine their artistic skills with their writing as they make a tourist guidebook.

Key points

Make sure students choose to write about a single event that happened at one place and time, such as an accident, party, ceremony, etc. A childhood memory works well.

Students could draw pictures of the scene of their event to help them think of vocabulary and descriptions.

Although the activities guide the students to think about places and events that happened close to their home, students could also write about events that happened in more distant places.

If you choose to do the *Just for fun* activity, bring in some English language tourist brochures for students to look at.

Useful language for this unit includes past tenses; the prepositions of place *in*, *on*, and *at*; and time expressions.

Sections can be skipped. A minimal set of sections might include Parts 4, 5, 6, and 7.

1 Brainstorming page 11

Tell students that they will brainstorm places near their homes where something special or interesting happened to them.

1

- Read the instructions for Step 1 aloud. Read the words in the box aloud and have the class repeat. Explain vocabulary as necessary.

- Have students complete 1a–f individually and then compare answers with a partner.
- Call on students to give the answers.

> **Answers**
> 1. a. a school
>   b. my friend's apartment
>   c. a store
>   d. a soccer field
>   e. a park
>   f. a river

2

- Call on a student to remind the class what brainstorming is (a method of finding ideas). Explain that writing lists is another method of brainstorming.
- Write the following headings on the board: *Important place* and *What happened?*
- Read the instructions for Step 2 aloud.
- Elicit some examples from students and write them on the board. (Possible examples: *playground – broke my arm*; *park near my house – learned to ride a bicycle*.)
- Have students brainstorm to complete the lists individually. Set a time limit of five minutes.
- Walk around the classroom, encouraging and helping students as necessary.

3

- Read the instructions for Step 3 aloud.
- Have students compare lists with a partner and add more ideas to their own lists.
- Call on some students to read their lists of ideas aloud to the class or write them on the board.

Later in this unit . . . Call on a student to read this aloud.

2 Analyzing a paragraph page 12

Tell students they will look at some typical sentences from a personal story.

1

- Read the instructions for Step 1 aloud.
- Call on students to tell you what they see in the picture. Provide vocabulary as necessary.
- Read the instructions for 1a–c aloud. Remind students that the topic is the most general subject of the paragraph.
- Have students complete 1a–c individually.

2

- Have students compare answers with a partner.
- Call on a student to read the answer to 1a aloud. Call on students to write the answers for 1b–c on the board.

> **Talk about it.** Read this aloud and have students talk with their partners for about five minutes.

3 Learning about organization page 13

- Tell students they will learn how to describe the scene of a personal story.
- Read the information box *Setting the scene* at the top of page 13.

1

- Read the instructions for Step 1 aloud.
- Focus students' attention on the picture. Ask them to tell you what they see.
- Read the Word File aloud. Explain vocabulary as necessary.
- Have students complete 1a–d individually and then compare answers in small groups.
- Go over answers as a whole class. Write the answers on the board.

2

- Read the instructions for Step 2 aloud.
- Read the Word File aloud. Explain vocabulary as necessary.
- Have students complete Step 2 individually.
- Call on individual students to write the sentences on the board.
- Go over answers as a whole class.

Optional activity

Partner writing

Have students work with a partner to write a short story using the expressions in the Word File in Step 2. They can work together on each sentence or take turns writing sentences. Encourage them to be creative!

---

4 Working on content page 14

Tell students they will choose an event and place to write about and then brainstorm ideas to write about.

1

- Read the instructions for Step 1 aloud.
- Call on individual students to read the example notes.

2

- Read the instructions for Step 2 aloud.
- Write the following on the board (as it appears in the text): *An important place*; *When did something important happen?*; *What happened?*
- Give students a few minutes to look back at their lists from Part 1 and choose a place and event to write about.
- Have students complete notes for themselves individually. Walk around the classroom, helping students as necessary.

3

- Read the instructions for Step 3 and the questions aloud.
- Have students work in groups of three to ask and answer questions about their important place and event.
- After about 15 minutes, or after everyone has had a chance to speak, call on groups to give examples of what students said.
- Ask the class questions, such as *What was the funniest / most unusual story you heard?* Write the examples on the board, filling in the chart. Alternatively, call students in turn to the board to fill out the chart.

5 Learning more about organization
page 15

- Tell students they will learn how to write an ending for their stories.
- Read the information box *Ending a personal story* at the top of page 15.
- Explain vocabulary as necessary.

1

- Read the instructions for Step 1 aloud.
- Call on a student to read the information in the box aloud. Explain vocabulary as necessary.
- Have students complete 1a–d with a partner.
- Go over answers as a whole class.

2

- Read the instructions for Step 2 aloud.
- Have students complete Step 2 individually. Set a time limit of 10 minutes.
- If students are having difficulty, elicit examples from one or two students and write them on the board.
- Walk around the classroom, helping students as necessary.
- Call on students to write their story endings on the board or read them aloud. Make corrections as necessary.

Optional activity

Vocabulary building

Write some more adjectives of feeling on the board, such as *disappointed, unhappy, satisfied, delighted, overjoyed*. Have students work with a partner to use their dictionaries to look up the meanings. Then have them come up with concluding sentences, as in Step 1 on page 15, that show the meanings of these words.

6 Analyzing a model   page 16

Tell students they will use the information they brainstormed in Parts 1–5 to write their stories.

1

- Read the instructions for Step 1 aloud.
- Have students read the paragraph individually. Remind them that they have read notes for this paragraph in previous sections.

- Call on students to read the paragraph aloud, sentence by sentence. Explain vocabulary as necessary.
- Have students complete 1a–e individually.

2

- Read the instructions for Step 2 aloud.
- Have students compare answers with a partner.
- Go over answers as a whole class.

7 Write! page 17

1

- Read the instructions for Steps 1 and 1a–c aloud.
- Set a time limit of 5 to 10 minutes for students to draw the picture or map.
- Have students go on to Steps 1b and 1c when they have finished drawing.
- Walk around the classroom, helping students as necessary.

2

- Read the instructions for Step 2 aloud.
- Have students write their paragraph on lined paper or type it. Have them skip lines. Tell them you'll collect the paragraphs after they're revised in Parts 8 and 9.

> **In your journal . . .** If time permits, read the journal entry instructions aloud. Tell students to use language from the first Word File in Part 3, if they can. Students can write in class or at home.

8 Editing page 18

- Tell students they will learn to use prepositional phrases to add more details to a story.
- Read the information box *Using prepositions* at the top of page 18.

1

- Read the instructions for Step 1 aloud.
- Have a student read the example sentences aloud. Explain vocabulary as necessary. If students have questions about the prepositions, draw pictures on the board to explain them.
- Have students complete Step 1 individually and then compare answers with a partner.
- Check answers by calling on students to read the sentences aloud.

2

- Read the instructions for Step 2 aloud.
- Have students complete Step 2 in class or at home.
- Call on students who made changes to their paragraphs to write their original sentences and their revisions on the board.

> ### Optional activity
>
> #### Group story writing
>
> Have students work in groups. Have them make a list of five to seven prepositional phrases. Each group passes their phrases to the next group, which collectively writes a short story incorporating as many of the phrases as possible. Groups read their stories aloud to the class. Encourage students to be creative!

9 Giving feedback page 19

Tell students that they are going to read each other's paragraphs and that they will need a sheet of paper for Step 2.

1

- Read the instructions for Steps 1 and 1a–b aloud.
- Have students exchange their paragraphs with a partner and complete 1a–b individually. Walk around the classroom, helping students as necessary.
- When they finish, tell them to exchange books and review their partner's answers. They can then go on to Step 2.

2

- Read the instructions for Step 2 aloud. Then call on a student to read the example letter.
- Have students write their letters to their partner individually.
- Walk around the classroom, helping students as necessary.

3

- Read the instructions for Step 3 aloud.
- Have students give their letters to their partner.
- Give students time to tell their partner the answer to any questions in the letter.
- Have students revise their paragraphs based on the comments they receive and other ideas they have. They can complete their revisions either in class or at home.
- Have students turn in their revised paragraphs to you.

Just for fun page 20

- Ask students: *How many of you like to travel? How many of you have used a guidebook?*
- Tell students that they are going to write a guidebook for their hometown or the town they're currently living in.

1

- Read the instructions for Step 1 aloud, including the examples in the chart.
- Have students brainstorm a list of activities in groups. All students should think of ideas, and one secretary in each group can write them down.
- Walk around the classroom, helping students as necessary.
- Write three columns titled *Children*, *Teenagers*, and *Adults* on the board. Write or have a student write some of the answers that the groups suggest.

> **Answers will vary. Possible answers:**
>
> *Children:* (a) Play on the playground equipment in the park. (b) Climb on the rocks around the lake. (c) Visit the children's museum downtown.
>
> *Teenagers:* (a) Go to the video arcade. (b) Go to the movie theater. (c) Play mini-golf.
>
> *Adults:* (a) Have coffee with your friends. (b) Eat delicious snacks. (c) Look at the local artwork in the village gallery.

2

- Read the instructions for Step 2 and the example sentences aloud.
- Have students take turns writing sentences for the guidebook. Alternatively, have all students think of sentences while one secretary writes them down.

3

- Read the instructions for Step 3 aloud. Use the pictures to explain the instructions.
- Have a student demonstrate how to fold the paper while you read the instructions.
- Have students complete their guidebooks in class or at home. Encourage them to be creative.

4

- Have each group give a presentation about their guidebooks. You may want to hang up the guidebooks to display in the classroom or share them with another class.

3 An ideal partner

Overview

In this unit, students write a paragraph about the kind of person they would like as a partner. They learn how to put information in order and give reasons.

In the prewriting activities, students describe preferences, values, and personality characteristics. They learn to support their opinions by giving reasons and to organize information in a paragraph with transition words such as *first*, *second*, and *third*. In Part 7, students combine their work from the prewriting activities into a paragraph. The postwriting editing activity on parallel structure helps students combine sentences to make their writing more interesting. The *Just for fun* activity has students review writing about people with an enjoyable game.

Key points

This unit is rich in vocabulary to describe personalities and characteristics. Encourage students to learn additional words that are meaningful to them.

If describing a romantic partner is inappropriate for some or all of your class, make the partner a business partner, roommate, or friend instead.

Useful language for this unit includes *I want a partner who (is tall)*, *I want a partner who (is tall) because (I am tall)*, and *I would like*.

Sections can be skipped. A minimal set of sections might include Parts 3, 4, 5, 6, and 7.

1 Brainstorming page 21

Before doing Step 1, define *ideal partner*. Tell the class: *An ideal partner is someone who is – or would be – perfect for you. It is someone you would like to be romantically involved with, like a boyfriend or girlfriend, or a husband or wife.*

1

- Read the instructions for Step 1 aloud. Explain that *characteristics* refer to what a person is like. Write these examples on the board: *is intelligent*, *has a good sense of humor*, *is hardworking*.
- Call on a student to read the six characteristics aloud. Explain vocabulary as necessary.

- Have students complete Step 1 individually.
- Have students compare answers in small groups or with a partner.
- Go over answers as a whole class by asking, *Is (being good-looking) an important characteristic in an ideal partner?* and have students raise their hands.

2

- Read the instructions for Step 2 aloud.
- Have students brainstorm individually. Set a time limit of three to five minutes.
- Walk around the classroom, helping students as necessary. You may need to provide additional vocabulary.

3

- Read the instructions for Step 3 aloud.
- Have students compare lists with a partner and add more ideas to their own lists.
- Call on some students to read their lists of ideas aloud to the class or write them on the board.

> **Later in this unit . . .** Call on a student to read this aloud.

2 Analyzing a paragraph page 22

1

- Read the instructions for Step 1 aloud.
- Have students read the paragraph individually.
- Call on students to read the paragraph aloud, sentence by sentence. Provide vocabulary as necessary.
- Read the instructions for 1a–d aloud.
- Have students complete 1a–d individually or with a partner.
- If students are having difficulty, you may want to stop after 1b and go over the answers.
- Ask students to raise their hands or nod at you to let you know when they have finished.

2

- Have students compare answers with a partner.
- Write or have individual students write answers on the board. Point out the commas after *First*, *Second*, and *Third*.

Talk about it. Read this aloud and have students talk with their partners for about five minutes.

Optional activity

Substitution game

Write the paragraph on the board with the following words underlined:

What kind of partner do I want? First, I want a partner who can <u>speak English</u>. Second, I want a partner who <u>likes to go to parties</u> because <u>I am very outgoing</u>. Third, I would like someone who likes to <u>travel</u>.

Have students take turns reading the sentences aloud, substituting different words for the underlined ones. If necessary, prepare by brainstorming a list of common likes with the whole class.

3 Working on content page 23

Tell students they will interview a classmate to find out about his or her ideal partner.

1

- Read the instructions for Step 1 aloud.
- Have a student read the example interview aloud.

2

- Read the instructions for Step 2 aloud.

- Read the characteristics in 2a–j aloud and have the class repeat. Check understanding of the vocabulary by eliciting definitions or examples from students. Explain vocabulary as necessary.
- Model the interview by calling on two students. Say, *Maria, ask Nina the first question.* Maria asks, *Nina, do you prefer a partner who is playful or who is serious?* Nina responds, *I want a partner who is serious*, and marks her own answer on the chart.
- Have students complete the interview with a classmate.
- Walk around the classroom, helping students as necessary.

3

- Read the instructions for Step 3 aloud.
- Have students stand up and talk to several other classmates.
- After 5 to 10 minutes, have students return to their seats and write their answer.
- Ask students about the responses they got from their classmates. You might ask, *Which response was most interesting to you?* or *Which response surprised you the most?*
- Call on volunteers to write their sentences on the board. While they are writing, walk around the room and check the sentences that the others wrote.

Optional activity

Class survey: The top five characteristics we want!

Write *Our ideal partner* on the board. Ask students to brainstorm the most important characteristics of an ideal partner and write them on the board. Have students vote for their favorites. Mark their answers and circle the five most popular characteristics. Then, as a class, write sentences about the class ideal partner (e.g., We would like someone who has a great job, is athletic, likes dancing, etc.). You may want to make separate lists for men and women.

4 Learning about organization page 24

- Read the information box *Listing points* at the top of page 24.
- Explain vocabulary as necessary.

1

- Read the instructions for Step 1 aloud.
- Call on a student to read the paragraph aloud. Explain vocabulary as necessary.
- Have students complete Step 1 individually.
- Call on students to read their answers. Write or have a student write the sentences on the board. If possible, use a colored marker or piece of chalk to insert *First*, *Second*, and *Third*.

> **Answer**
>
> 1. What kind of partner do I want? **First,** I want a partner who likes movies. **Second,** I would like a partner who likes to dance. I love music and dancing. **Third,** I would like a partner who thinks family is important. My family is important to me.

2

- Read the instructions for Step 2 aloud.
- Point out that in this situation, *want* and *would like* have the same meaning. Students should use both expressions to add variety to their writing.
- Have students complete 2a–c individually.
- Call on students to share their examples with the class by reading them aloud or writing them on the board.

> **Answers will vary. Possible answers:**
>
> 2. a. is ambitious: I want a partner who is ambitious.
>   b. can dance: I would like a partner who can dance.
>   c. likes children: I prefer a partner who likes children.

3

- Read the instructions for Step 3 aloud.
- Tell students to write the most important characteristic first, the next most important characteristic second, etc.
- Have students complete Step 3 individually. Walk around the classroom, helping them as necessary.

> **Answers will vary. Possible answer:**
>
> 3. First, I want a partner who is ambitious. Second, I would like a partner who can dance. Third, I prefer a partner who likes children.

5 Learning more about organization
page 25

- Tell students that giving support – more information, explanations, and details – makes their writing stronger.
- Read the information box *Adding reasons* at the top of page 25.
- Have another student read the example. Explain that what comes after *because* supports what came before it by giving a reason. This helps readers understand your ideas more easily.

1

- Read the instructions for Step 1 aloud.
- Have students individually complete 1a–d. For lower-level classes, do 1a together as a class and write the answer on the board.
- Go over answers as a whole class. Write or have individual students write the sentences on the board. Ask, *Does anyone have similar interests or desires for his or her partner?*

> **Answers**
>
> 1. a. I would like a partner who is serious about school because I like people with a good education.
>   b. I prefer a partner who likes sports because I play tennis a lot.
>   c. I want a partner who doesn't tell lies because I had a partner once who lied to me and hurt my feelings.
>   d. I want a partner who likes children because I want to have a big family.

2

- Read the instructions for Step 2 aloud.
- Have students complete 2a–c individually.
- Walk around the classroom, helping students as necessary.
- Have volunteers write their sentences on the board or read them aloud.

Group review

Have students work in small groups. Have each student share the sentences they wrote in Step 2. As a group, have them vote on their favorite sentence. (It could be the most interesting because it's funny, unusual, surprising, etc.) Have a representative from each group write the sentence on the board and explain to the class why they thought it was interesting.

6 Analyzing a model page 26

1

- Read the instructions for Step 1 aloud.
- Have students read the paragraph individually.
- Call on students to read the paragraph aloud. Explain vocabulary as necessary.
- Have students complete 1a–c individually or with a partner.

Answers

1. a. First; Second; Third
   b. likes sports; likes being with groups of people; likes to travel
   c. I would like; I enjoy; I love

2

- Have students compare answers with a partner.
- Go over answers as a whole class.

7 Write! page 27

1

- Read the instructions for Step 1 aloud, including those for 1a–c.
- Have students complete 1a–c individually. Remind them that they have discussed and written the information in previous sections. However, they may write new information if they wish.
- Walk around the classroom, helping students as necessary.

2

- Have students write their paragraph on lined paper or type it. Have them skip lines.
- Tell them you'll collect the paragraphs after they're revised in Parts 8 and 9.

In your journal . . . If time permits, read the journal entry instructions aloud. Tell students they can write about different ideas for the ideal day as well. Have them use the structures *I want to* and *I would like to*. Students can write in class or at home.

8 Editing page 28

- Tell students that we often combine sentences when possible to make writing more interesting.
- Read the information box *Combining sentences* at the top of page 28.
- Point out how the sentences that are combined are ones with similar structures.

1

- Read the instructions for Step 1 aloud.
- Call on a student to read the paragraph aloud. Explain vocabulary as necessary.
- Have students complete Step 1 individually. Remind them to look for sentences next to each other that have the same verbs.
- Go over answers as a whole class.

Answers

1. I like swimming. I also like sailing. I also like surfing.
   I prefer staying at home with my partner. I prefer being alone with my partner.
   I like watching TV with my partner. I also like listening to music with my partner.
   Third, I hope my partner is a good listener. I hope my partner can understand my problems. I also hope my partner can give me advice.
   I like people who think about life's problems. I like people who discuss such problems.

2

- Read the instructions for Step 2 and the example sentence aloud.

- Have students complete 2a–e individually or with a partner. If students work with a partner, have them decide on an answer together, and then have each write the answer in his or her book.

- Go over answers by having students come to the board and write the answers.

> **Answers**
>
> 2. a. I like swimming, sailing, and surfing.
>   b. I prefer staying at home (with) and being alone with my partner.
>   c. I like watching TV and listening to music with my partner.
>   d. Third, I hope my partner is a good listener, can understand my problems, and can give me advice.
>   e. I like people who think about life's problems and discuss such problems. / I like people who think about and discuss life's problems.

3

- Read the instructions for Step 3 aloud.

- Have students who want to combine sentences revise their paragraphs from Part 7 in class or at home.

- Have students share their revisions in groups or have volunteers write their old and new sentences on the board.

9 Giving feedback page 29

Tell students that they are going to read each other's paragraphs and that they will need a sheet of paper for Step 2.

1

- Read the instructions for Steps 1 and 1a–c aloud.

- Have students exchange their paragraphs with a classmate and complete 1a–c individually. Walk around the classroom, helping students as necessary.

- When they finish, ask the class, *How many people checked (artist)?* See which was the most popular partner chosen. Ask how many people wrote their own ideas, and what they were.

- Tell students to exchange books and review their classmate's answers.

2

- Read the instructions for Step 2 aloud. Then call on a student to read the example letter.

- Have students write their letters to their partner individually.

- Walk around the classroom, helping students as necessary.

3

- Read the instructions for Step 3 aloud.

- Have students give their letters to their partner.

- Have students revise their paragraphs based on the comments they receive and other ideas they have. They can complete their revisions either in class or at home.

- Have students turn in their revised paragraphs to you.

Just for fun page 30

- If you have a large class, divide them into smaller groups of 8 to 10 students to play the game.

- A table or group of flat desks pushed together is useful.

- Tell students that they will need a sheet of paper for Step 1.

- Ask, *Do you know what a dating game is?* Have students who have seen dating games on TV describe them to the class.

1

- Read the instructions for Steps 1 and 1a–d aloud.

- Point out the model character profile sheet.

- Have students complete 1a–d individually or with a partner.

- Make sure each group is creating an equal number of male and female characters. If necessary, assign a gender to each student's or pair's character.

- Walk around the classroom, encouraging and helping students as necessary.

2

- Read the instructions for Step 2a aloud and have students carry them out before you continue.

- Read the instructions for 2b–c aloud and answer any questions before continuing. To check comprehension, ask a student to explain the instructions again.

- Give students about 10 minutes to read the character profiles and write down who they think would best match their character. If students created a character with a partner, the pair makes this decision together.

3

- Have each student (or one student from each pair) point to the partner his or her character chose.
- Ask the groups if there were any matches.
- Have students role-play their characters. Have the matched couples explain why they chose each other, and ask a few characters who couldn't get partners for comments about their choices.

Optional activity

Letter to an ideal partner

Have students write a letter that the character they created might send to his or her desired partner in the game (even if they did not become a couple). Encourage students to have fun with this not-so-serious activity. They can use sentences similar to the ones they wrote in their paragraph. Have the groups deliver their letters.

4 My favorite photo

Overview

In this unit, students write a paragraph to describe one of their favorite photos. In addition, they learn how to begin and end their paragraph.

In the prewriting activities, students learn to begin a paragraph with general information, add supporting sentences that give details about their photos, and write a concluding sentence that summarizes the paragraph. In the postwriting activity, students decide whether information in their paragraph should be written in the present or the past tense. The *Just for fun* activity lets students extend and develop the skills they practiced in the unit by writing about several important events in their life.

Key points

Remember to tell students beforehand to bring two or three of their favorite photos to class to use in Part 3 and afterward. They can use the photos in their phones/cameras, but it's best to have them on paper. Have students who forget to bring photos (or don't have any) to draw pictures.

Encourage students to choose photos where something is happening. They should know the people in the photo well enough to write about them.

Useful language for this unit includes the simple present and simple past tenses.

Sections can be skipped. A minimal set of sections might include Parts 3, 4, 5, 6, and 7.

1 Brainstorming page 31

1

- Read the instructions for Step 1 aloud.
- Call on students to read the captions from the photo album. Explain vocabulary as necessary by using the pictures.
- Have students complete Step 1 individually.
- Go over responses as a whole class by reading each caption and having students raise their hand if they checked it.

2

- Read the instructions for Step 2 aloud. Point out that students can write notes instead of complete sentences.
- Have students complete Step 2 individually. Set a time limit of three to five minutes.

3

- Read the instructions for Step 3 aloud.
- Have students compare lists with a partner and add more ideas to their own lists.
- Call on some students to read their list of ideas aloud to the class or write them on the board.

> **Later in this unit . . .** Call on a student to read this aloud.

Optional activity

Class survey of popular photos

Have students work in groups. Have one person be the group's secretary. Have students make a list of types of photos that they all have (e.g., a high school graduation, birthday party, etc.) and then guess what the five most popular class photos are. Check answers by calling on students from each group to write their lists and guesses on the board. See which group had the most accurate list of the class's five most popular photos.

2 Analyzing a paragraph page 32

1

- Read the instructions for Step 1 aloud.
- Have students read the paragraph individually.
- Call on students to read the paragraph aloud, sentence by sentence. Explain vocabulary as necessary.
- Read the instructions for 1a–d aloud.
- Have students complete 1a–d individually.

- Walk around the classroom, helping students as necessary.
- If your students are having a difficult time, you may want to stop after lb and review.
- Ask students to raise their hands or nod at you when they have finished.

Answers

1. a. my friends and me; on my twenty-first birthday
   b. I like this photo because it reminds me of a very special day.
   c. My favorite photo is of my family and me on New Year's Day.
   d. It was taken when I was 16 at my grandmother's house.

2

- Have students compare answers with a partner.
- Call on students to write the answers on the board.

Talk about it. Read this aloud and have students talk with their partners for about five minutes.

Optional activity

Photo album

Have students bring in a photo album to show classmates. Divide the class into small groups. Have students take turns showing a few photos from their albums. Tell students to use the language in Part 2 to discuss their photos. Group members can ask questions about the photos. After about 10 minutes, call on students to tell the class what they learned about their classmates.

3 Working on content page 33

1

- Read the instructions for Step 1 aloud.
- Call on individual students to read the *who*, *what*, *when*, and *where* information about Wes's photo aloud.

2

- Read the instructions for Step 2 aloud.
- If students did not bring photos to class, have them draw pictures or use their imagination.
- Ask, *Why are the details important?* (Possible answers: because they make the descriptions more interesting; because they add information)
- Have students complete their charts individually. Walk around the classroom, helping students as necessary.
- If students are having difficulty, draw the chart on the board, call a student to the board, and complete the chart together.
- Walk around the classroom, encouraging and helping students as necessary. You may want to take additional class time to correct errors with individual sentences, or you can have students compare their answers with a partner.

3

- Read the instructions for Step 3 aloud.
- Have students work with a partner to ask and answer questions about their charts.
- Walk around the classroom, encouraging and helping students as necessary.
- Give students time to add information to their charts.
- Review as a class. Call on students to share the examples they wrote.

Optional activity

Match the photo

Bring in photos from magazines or the Internet of famous people or people doing interesting things. Have students work with a partner. Give each pair one or two photos. Have each pair write a general sentence that describes the photo on a slip of paper. They should use their imagination. Post the photos around the room. Collect the sentences, mix them up, and give a new one to each pair. Have pairs stand up and move around the room to find the photo that matches their sentence. The first pair to find the match wins.

4 Learning about organization page 34

- Read the information box *Giving background information* at the top of page 34.
- Tell students that they are now going to build on the ideas discussed in Part 3.

1

- Read the instructions for Step 1 aloud, noting the *wh-*word that students will use in each example: *who* or *what*, *when*, and *where*.
- Call on individual students to read the examples aloud.
- Read the instructions for 1a–c.
- Have students complete 1a–c individually.
- Walk around the classroom, encouraging and helping students as necessary.

> **Optional activity**
>
> **Boring or exciting?**
>
> Have students work with a partner. Give each pair a photo. (You can use students' photos or the pictures from the Optional Activity in Part 3.) Tell pairs to write two descriptions for each photo: one that's boring and one that's exciting. Then have pairs read their descriptions to the class. The class says which description is boring and which description is exciting. Encourage students to read with expression.

5 Learning more about organization

page 35

- Read the information box *Writing a concluding sentence* at the top of page 35.
- Call on a student to read the examples aloud.

1

- Read the instructions for Step 1 aloud.
- Call on students to read the choices for 1a–d aloud. Explain vocabulary as necessary.
- Have students work with a partner to complete 1a–d.
- Go over answers as a whole class. Discuss why the other sentences are not good concluding sentences.

Answers

1. a. I like this photo because our trip to the Grand Canyon was wonderful.
   b. This photo reminds me of the trips I took with that good friend.
   c. When I look at this photo, I remember our wonderful concert.
   d. This photo helps me remember the years I lived in Japan.

2

- Read the instruction for Step 2 aloud.
- Have students complete Step 2 individually. Walk around the classroom, helping students as necessary.
- Have students compare sentences with a partner.
- Call on some students to write their sentences on the board.

> **Optional activity**
>
> **Concluding sentences about paintings**
>
> Bring in copies of several paintings from magazines or the Internet. If your students are imaginative, use abstract as well as representational paintings. Have students work with a partner. Give each pair a painting (you can give a copy of the same painting to more than one pair). Have students write a concluding sentence like the ones in Part 5 about the painting. Write this useful language on the board:
>
> *What does this painting remind you of?*
> *I like this painting because it reminds me of . . .*
> *This painting helps me to remember . . .*
> *When I look at this painting, I remember . . .*
>
> Encourage students to be creative! Have pairs share their sentences with other pairs.

6 Analyzing a model page 36

1

- Read the instructions for Step 1 aloud.
- Ask, *What do you see in the photo?* Provide vocabulary as necessary.
- Have students read the paragraph individually.

- Call on students to read the paragraph aloud. Explain vocabulary as necessary.
- Read the instructions for 1a–c aloud.
- Have students complete 1a–c individually.

2

- Read the instructions for Step 2 aloud. Have students compare answers with a partner.
- Go over answers as a whole class.

7 Write! page 37

1

- Read the instructions for Steps 1 and 1a–d aloud.
- Have students complete a–d individually. Tell them to use the information they wrote in Parts 3–5.
- Walk around and help students as necessary.

2

- Read the instructions for Step 2 aloud.
- Have students write their paragraph on lined paper or type it. Have them skip lines. Tell them you'll collect the paragraphs after they're revised in Parts 8 and 9.

> In your journal . . . If time permits, read the journal entry instructions aloud. If students don't have a camera, they can write about why they don't have a camera or about the kind of photos or artwork they like to look at. Students can write in class or at home.

8 Editing page 38

Read the information box *Mixing past and present tense* at the top of page 38.

1

- Ask, *What do you see in the photo?* Provide vocabulary as necessary.
- Read the instructions for Step 1 aloud.
- Call on students to read the paragraph aloud, with the verbs in the base form. Explain vocabulary as necessary.
- Have students complete Step 1 individually or with a partner.
- Check answers by calling on students to read the sentences aloud.

2

- Read the instructions for Step 2 aloud.
- Have students check their paragraphs from Part 7 in class or at home and revise as necessary.
- Have students share their revisions in groups or have volunteers write their old and new sentences on the board.

9 Giving feedback page 39

Tell students that they are going to read each other's paragraphs and that they will need a sheet of paper for Step 2.

1

- Read the instructions for Steps 1 and 1a–b aloud.
- Have students exchange their paragraphs with a partner and complete 1a–b individually. Walk around the classroom, helping students as necessary.
- Tell students to exchange books and review their partner's answers.

2

- Read the instructions for Step 2 aloud. Then call on a student to read the example letter.
- Have students work individually to write their letters to their partner.
- Walk around the classroom, helping students as necessary.

3

- Read the instructions for Step 3 aloud.
- Have students give their letters to their partner. Give them time to tell their partner the answer to the question in the letter.
- Have students revise their paragraphs based on the comments they receive and other ideas they have. They can complete their revisions either in class or at home.
- Have students turn in their revised paragraphs to you.

Optional activity

Class photo gallery

Set up a display area on a wall either in the classroom or in the hall. Have students bring in another favorite photo to write about. Have them write sentences or paragraphs about the photos on index cards. Put interested students in charge of creating the display.

Just for fun page 40

- Tell students they will use photos to create a time line of their lives.
- If students don't have childhood photos, they can draw pictures.
- Students will need large pieces of paper or poster board and colored pencils or markers.

1

- Read the instructions for Step 1 aloud.
- Call on different students to read the information in the time line aloud. Explain vocabulary as necessary.

2

- Read the instructions for Step 2 aloud.
- Have students complete the chart individually.

3

- Read the instructions for Step 3 aloud.
- Distribute poster paper to the class.
- Have students complete Step 3 individually.

4

- Read the instructions for Step 4 aloud.
- Call on a student to read the example aloud.
- Have students write their descriptions individually.
- Walk around the classroom, helping students as necessary.

5

- Read the instructions for Step 5 aloud.
- Have students take turns explaining their time lines to the class.
- Ask students what interesting things they learned about each other.

Optional activity

Writing about classmates

Have students write in their journals about their classmates' time lines. They can answer the following questions: What was the most surprising thing you learned about your classmates? Which one was most similar to yours? Explain!

5 *My seal*

Overview

In this unit, students design a personal seal and write a paragraph explaining the position and meaning of the symbols they chose. They also learn how to write topic sentences.

In the prewriting activities, students brainstorm symbols that represent their interests and personalities. They use prepositions of place to describe the organization of their seals. The central writing assignment of the unit in Part 7 combines their drawn seal with a written description. The postwriting activity shows students how to move clauses with *because* to the beginning of a sentence to add variety to their writing. The *Just for fun* activity gives students further practice with the same concepts and language as they design a flag with their group.

Key points

Bring some seals, flags, or logos to the first class. Show how they are made of symbols. You can use seals from companies, political organizations, sports teams, etc. Many of these can be found on the Internet.

Some students might take a long time to design their seal, so leave ample class time or assign the seal design as homework.

If students draw their seals in class, ask them to bring colored pencils or markers.

Useful language for this unit includes prepositions of place and the connector *because*.

Sections can be skipped. A minimal set of sections might include Parts 4, 5, 6, and 7.

1 Brainstorming page 41

1

- Read the instructions for Step 1 aloud. Ask students to tell you what they see in the seal. Provide vocabulary as necessary.
- Read the information in the box and sentences in 1a–d aloud.
- Have students complete Step 1 individually and then compare answers with a partner.
- Go over answers as a whole class.

Answers
1. a. strength
   b. study
   c. sports
   d. people from many cultures

2

- Read the instructions for Step 2 aloud.
- Call on a student to read the different categories and examples in the chart aloud.
- Have students complete Step 2 individually. Set a time limit of five minutes.
- Walk around the classroom, helping students as necessary.

3

- Read the instructions for Step 3 aloud.
- Have students compare lists with a partner and add more ideas to their own lists.
- Call on some students to read their list of ideas aloud to the class or write them on the board.

> **Later in this unit . . .** Call on a student to read this aloud.

2 Analyzing a paragraph page 42

1

- Read the instructions for Step 1 aloud.
- Have students read the paragraph individually.
- Call on students to read the paragraph aloud, sentence by sentence. Have the rest of the class point to the symbol on the seal as the appropriate sentence is read. Explain vocabulary as necessary.
- Point out the colon [:] in sentence 1. This punctuation mark shows that an example or explanation will follow. A guitar and four stars are examples of two symbols.
- Read the instructions for 1a–d aloud.
- Have students complete 1a–d individually.

- Walk around the classroom, helping students as necessary.
- Ask students to raise their hands or nod to let you know when they have finished.

2

- Have students compare answers with a partner.
- Elicit answers from the class.
- Call on students to write the sentences from 1a–d on the board. Check to see that a colon was used in 1b.
- Point out the use of commas in a list of three items, as in 1b (a pen, a rose, and two hearts).

Answers

1. a. guitar; my hobby, playing pop music / four stars; my four best friends
   b. My seal has three symbols: a pen, a rose, and two hearts.
   c. The pen represents my dream, becoming a writer.
   d. The rose and two hearts represent my wife and our two children. or The rose represents my wife, and the two hearts represent our two children.

Talk about it. Read this aloud and have students talk with their partners for about five minutes.

Optional activity

Sports team symbols

Have students work in small groups. Have them brainstorm five different sports teams with symbols or logos they know. Write this pattern on the board as a model: *The symbol of the soccer team Real Madrid is a crown. We think the crown represents power.* Groups may need to use dictionaries or ask you for help with vocabulary. Artistic students could draw pictures of the symbols as well. When they are finished, have each group present their ideas to the class. Do the other class members agree with the interpretation? When all the groups are finished, ask students which symbols they like the best.

3 Working on content page 43

1

- Read the instructions for Step 1 aloud.
- Call on students to read the examples in the chart aloud. Explain vocabulary as necessary.

2

- Read the instructions for Step 2 aloud.
- Have students complete Step 2 individually.
- Walk around the classroom, helping students as necessary. Students may need to use their dictionaries or ask your help to find the name of the plant or animal they want.

3

- Read the instructions for Step 3 aloud.
- Call on two students to read the model interview aloud.
- Give students some time to plan what they are going to say.
- Have students interview each other, using the model as a guide.
- Call on students to share the information they learned in the interview.
- Point out that they are writing down the same information they gave in their interviews.

4

- Read the instructions for Step 4 aloud.
- Have students complete Step 4 individually.
- Walk around the classroom, helping students as necessary.
- Call on some students to write their sentences on the board. Walk around the classroom to check other students' sentences.

4 Learning about organization page 44

- You may want to bring or ask students to bring colored pencils or markers to make their seals.
- Read the information box *Organizing information by location* at the top of page 44.

1

- Read the instructions for Steps 1 and 1a–b aloud.
- Have students complete 1a–b individually.

- Walk around the classroom, encouraging and helping students as necessary.
- If some students are reluctant to draw in their books, have them draw on a separate sheet of paper.
- Have students share their seals in small groups.

2

- Read the instructions for Step 2 aloud.
- Have students complete 2a–c individually.
- Go over answers as a whole class.

3

- Read the instructions for Step 3 aloud.
- Have students complete Step 3 individually.
- Have students compare answers with a partner. Walk around the classroom, helping students as necessary and checking their work.

Optional activity

Drawing your partner's seal

Have students work with a partner and take turns reading their sentences from Part 4, Step 3. They should not show their seal to their partner. Their partner listens to the sentences and draws the seal. When both partners have finished, have them compare the seals they drew. Were they similar? Students can also try to guess what their partner's symbols represent.

---

5 Learning more about organization
page 45

- Read the information box *Topic sentences* at the top of page 45.
- Call on a student to read the example aloud.
- Tell students that topic sentences help the writer create a more organized paragraph and also help the reader easily understand the writer's main idea.

1

- Read the instructions for Step 1 aloud.
- Have a student read the words from the box aloud. Explain vocabulary as necessary.
- Have students work with a partner to complete Step 1. Encourage students to guess, if they are not sure of the answer.
- Go over answers as a whole class.

2

- Read the instructions for Step 2 aloud.
- Call on students to read the three sentences aloud.
- Ask a volunteer which one would be the best topic sentence.
- Write the answer on the board and ask why the other answers would not be good topic sentences. (Answer: The other sentences don't introduce the main idea of this paragraph.)

3

- Read the instructions for Step 3 aloud.
- Have students complete Step 3 individually.
- Go over the answer as a whole class.
- Discuss with the class why the other sentences would not be good topic sentences for that paragraph.

4

- Read the instructions for Step 4 aloud.
- Have students work individually to write their sentences.
- Elicit examples from the class and write them on the board.

6 Analyzing a model page 46

1

- Read the instructions for Step 1 aloud.
- Ask students to tell you what they see in the seal. Provide vocabulary as necessary.
- Have students read the paragraph individually.
- Call on students to read the paragraph aloud. If necessary, use a world map to show where Costa Rica and Canada are.
- Read the instructions for 1a–c aloud.
- Have students complete 1a–c individually or with a partner.
- Go over answers as a whole class.

Answers

1. a. My seal has four symbols: a pine tree, wheels, a sun, and snow.
   b. in the center; below the tree; Above the tree on the right; on the left
   c. pine tree; a character that never changes

   wheels; my motorcycle

   sun; Costa Rica (where I was born)

   snow; Canada (where I live now)

2

- Read the instructions for Step 2 aloud.
- Go over answers as a whole class.

7 Write! page 47

1

- Tell students they will design their own personal seal.
- Read the instructions for Steps 1 and 1a–e aloud.
- Have students complete 1a–e individually.

2

- Read the instructions for Step 2 aloud.
- Have students write their paragraph on lined paper or type it. Have them skip lines. If they wish, they can draw their seal on a separate sheet and attach it. Tell them you'll collect the paragraphs after they're revised in Parts 8 and 9.

In your journal . . . If time permits, read the journal entry instructions aloud. Encourage students to use language from the unit if they can. They can also write about what different colors represent in their cultures (e.g., *In my country, purple represents royalty.*). Students can write in class or at home.

8 Editing page 48

- Read the information box *Commas with because* at the top of page 48.
- Write the word *because* on the board.
- Have students give you some example sentences using *because*. They could use examples from their paragraphs from Part 7.
- Explain that the position of *because* does not change the meaning of the sentence. Encourage students to use *because* in both positions to add variety to their writing.
- Read the second example sentence again, pausing after the first clause to demonstrate why a comma is used there.

1

- Read the instructions for Step 1 aloud.
- Have students complete 1a–f individually.
- Walk around the classroom, helping students as necessary.
- Have students compare answers with a partner.
- Go over answers as a whole class.

2

■ Read the instructions for Step 2 aloud.

■ Have students complete 2a–f with a partner.

■ Walk around the classroom, helping students as necessary.

■ Go over answers as a whole class.

3

■ Read the instructions for Step 3 aloud.

■ Have students check their paragraphs from Part 7 in class or at home and revise as necessary.

■ Have students share their revisions in groups, or have volunteers write their old and new sentences on the board.

9 Giving feedback page 49

Tell students that they are going to read four other students' paragraphs and that they will need a sheet of paper for Step 4.

1

■ Read the instructions for Step 1 aloud, including the chart.

■ Have students in one group of four exchange paragraphs with another group of four.

■ Have students read all four of the other group's paragraphs. They can take turns reading them aloud one by one, or read them silently and pass them around the group.

■ Give students time to discuss and complete the chart.

■ Walk around the classroom, helping students as necessary.

2

■ Read the instructions for Step 2 aloud.

■ Have each student choose just one paragraph to use for Steps 2, 3, and 4.

■ Have students complete Step 2 individually.

3

■ Read the instructions for Step 3 aloud.

■ Call on students to read the sentences in Step 3 aloud.

■ Have students complete Step 3 individually.

■ When students finish, tell them to exchange books and review their partner's answers. They can then go on to Step 4.

4

■ Read the instructions for Step 4 aloud. Then call on a student to read the example letter.

■ Have students write their letters to their partner individually.

■ Walk around the classroom, helping students as necessary.

■ Have students give their letters to their partner. Give them time to tell their partner the answer to the question in the letter.

5

- Read the instructions for Step 5 aloud.
- Have students revise their paragraphs based on the comments they receive and other ideas they have. They can complete their revisions either in class or at home.
- Have students turn in their revised paragraphs to you.

Just for fun page 50

- If you can, provide students with poster paper, markers or colored pencils, colored paper, scissors, and glue. You can also bring in old magazines for students to cut up for pictures.
- Encourage students to be creative!

1

- Read the instructions for Step 1 aloud.
- Have students work in small groups to choose a club or class as the subject for their flag.

2

- Read the instructions for Step 2 aloud.
- Read the words in the Word File aloud and have the class repeat. Explain vocabulary as necessary.
- Have students work in groups of four to complete Step 2. They can all work together on each symbol, or have two students work on one symbol and two students work on the other.
- Walk around the classroom, helping students as necessary.

3

- Read the instructions for Step 3 aloud.
- Have students work with their groups to complete Step 3. Remind groups to let all members participate equally.

4

- Read the instructions for Step 4 aloud.
- Suggest ways that groups can work together to complete the poster (e.g., different students can be in charge of drawing, coloring, writing, or directing the work).
- Give students time to plan their work.
- Have students work in groups to complete their posters.
- If necessary, write these phrases on the board so groups can borrow materials from each other: *May I borrow the (tape)? Can I use the (blue marker)? Sure, go ahead. I'm sorry, we're still using it.*
- Walk around the classroom, helping students as necessary.

5

- Read the instructions for Step 5 aloud.
- Have groups take turns explaining different parts, or select one member to make the presentation.
- After the presentations, hang the posters around the classroom.

6 Party time

Overview

In this unit, students plan a class party. They write an announcement and a paragraph describing their party plans, with details about time, place, and activities. They also learn to plan a paragraph by making a list.

The prewriting activities focus on brainstorming details about the party and organizing them in a clear and logical way. The main writing assignment in Part 7 shows students how to combine an announcement and a paragraph into one piece of writing. The postwriting activity shows students how to add an explanation to a suggestion by using *so that* and *to* to combine two sentences. The *Just for fun* activity teaches students some basic principles of graphic design as they create posters for their parties.

Key points

Encourage students to give sufficient details in their party plans. Remind them that anything they don't mention in their announcements and paragraphs can't be carried out.

After the party plans are finished, we suggest voting on one as a class to actually hold. You should set any limitations and requirements for the party (such as when and where the party could take place) in advance.

For the *Just for fun* activity, bring or ask students to bring sheets of poster paper, colored pencils and markers, old magazines to cut up, scissors, tape, and glue.

Useful language for this unit includes imperatives, *going to* and *will*, and *let's*.

Sections can be skipped. A minimal set of sections might include Parts 3, 4, 5, 6, and 7.

1 Brainstorming page 51

1

- Read the instructions for Step 1 aloud.
- Call on students to read the caption for each of the pictures. Explain vocabulary as necessary.
- Have students complete Step 1 individually.

- Go over responses as a whole class by reading each activity aloud and having students raise their hands if they would like to do the activity with the class.

2

- Read the instructions for Step 2 aloud.
- Have students complete Step 2 individually. Set a time limit of five minutes.
- Walk around the classroom, helping students as necessary.

3

- Read the instructions for Step 3 aloud.
- Have students compare lists with a partner and add more ideas to their own lists.
- Call on some students to read their lists of ideas aloud to the class or write them on the board.

> **Later in this unit . . .** Call on a student to read this aloud.

Optional activity

Brainstorming activities for other occasions

Write other occasions relevant to your students' lives on the board (e.g., *graduation* or *birthday party*). Have students work in groups to brainstorm activities for these occasions. Set a time limit of five to eight minutes. Ask groups to write their three best ideas on the board. Then have the class vote on the three best ideas overall.

---

2 Analyzing a paragraph page 52

1

- Read the instructions for Step 1 aloud.
- Ask students to tell you what they see in the picture. Provide vocabulary as necessary.
- Have students read the paragraph individually.
- Call on students to read the paragraph aloud, sentence by sentence. Point out the exclamation point, used here to mark exciting information.
- Read the instructions for 1a–d aloud.

- Have students complete 1a–d individually.
- If your students are having difficulty, you may want to stop after lb and review.
- Ask students to raise their hands or nod to let you know when they have finished.

2

- Have students compare answers with a partner.
- Go over answers as a whole class. Call on students to write the sentences for lc–d on the board. Check punctuation.

Answers

1. a. class hike
   b. Don't forget to bring a water bottle; We'll meet at Bell School at 6:50 a.m.
   c. Winter is coming, so let's go on a class ski trip!
   d. Wear a coat and gloves because it will (probably) be cold.

Talk about it. Read this aloud and have students talk with their partners for about five minutes.

Optional activity

What do we need?

With the class, brainstorm possible activities for a class trip (e.g., a hike, a trip to the beach, a camping trip). Divide the class into small groups and have each group brainstorm items they will need for one of the trips. Have them work together to write sentences like this: *Summer is coming, so let's go to the beach! Bring a big hat because the sun is strong.* When they finish, have one student from each group read their sentences to the class. Can the class think of anything they forgot to mention?

3 Working on content page 53

1

- Read the instructions for Step 1 aloud.
- Call on a student to read the information in the announcement aloud. Explain vocabulary as necessary.
- Have students complete Step 1 individually.
- Go over answers as a whole class.

Answers

1. a. June 1
   b. 11:00 a.m.
   c. free
   d. Andy
   e. in English class
   f. 12:10 p.m.

2

- Read the instructions for Step 2 aloud.
- Have students complete Step 2 individually. Encourage them to write about a party they really want to have, since these notes will be used for the main writing assignment.
- Walk around the classroom, helping students as necessary.
- Have students compare ideas with a partner.

3

- Read the instructions for Step 3 aloud. Remind students that a topic sentence gives general information about the paragraph.
- Call on a student to read the examples aloud.
- Have students complete Step 3 individually.
- Call on some students to write their topic sentences on the board. Walk around the classroom to check the other students' sentences.

4 Learning about organization page 54

- Read the information box *Plans and instructions* at the top of page 54.
- Call on students to read the example plans and instructions.
- Point out that the plans use *will* and the instructions use the imperative.

1

- Read the instructions for Step 1 aloud.
- Ask students to tell you what they see in the pictures. Provide vocabulary as necessary.
- Have students complete 1a–d individually. Point out that they should use the pictures to suggest what words to write.

- Walk around the classroom, helping students as necessary.
- Have students compare answers with a partner. Point out that all of the sentences are plans.

Answers

1. a. Bell School
   b. bus
   c. hike
   d. have a picnic

2

- Read the instructions for Step 2 and the Word File aloud.
- Have students complete Step 2 individually.
- Have students compare answers with a partner. Point out that all of the sentences are instructions.

Answers

2. d; Bring something to eat and drink.
   a; Please do not arrive late.
   c; Wear old clothes because you will get dirty.
   b; Please buy a bus ticket by Tuesday.

Optional activity

Party priorities

Have students work in small groups. Have them brainstorm for five minutes about what things are important for a great party (e.g., food, music, games). When they are done, call on groups to report their ideas and list all of them on the board. Then ask groups to choose the five most important things and rank them in order of importance, with 1 being the most important and 5 being the least important. When they are done, have each group present and explain their rankings to the class. Discuss differences of opinions as a whole class.

---

5 Working more on content   page 55

1

- Read the instructions for Step 1 aloud.
- Call on students to read the sample lists for *Before the party* and *At the party* aloud. Explain vocabulary as necessary.

2

- Read the instructions for Step 2 aloud.
- Have students complete Step 2 individually. Set a time limit of five to seven minutes.
- Walk around the classroom, helping students as necessary.
- Ask the class, *How is this kind of list like a brainstorm?* (Answer: It's like a brainstorm because you write words and phrases instead of sentences, and because you will get ideas that you can use to write a well-organized paragraph.)

3

- Read the instructions for Step 3 aloud.
- Have students complete Step 3 individually.
- Give students time to revise their lists as necessary. Remind them that the ideas they check will be the ones they include in their paragraphs.

4

- Read the instructions for Step 4 aloud.
- Have students show their lists (and party names) to a partner. Encourage them to explain why they did or didn't check each item.
- Encourage students to make any changes they'd like to make.

6 Analyzing a model   page 56

1

- Read the instructions for Step 1 aloud.
- Have students read the paragraph individually.
- Call on students to read the paragraph aloud, sentence by sentence. Explain vocabulary as necessary.
- Read the instructions for 1a–d aloud.
- Have students complete 1a–d individually.

Answers

1. a. Summer is coming, so let's celebrate with an "Aloha Friday" party!
   b. we are going to have a Hawaiian fashion contest; each person will walk in front of the room; choose the best Hawaiian look; we will eat some coconuts and drink pineapple juice; play my ukulele; teach the class a Hawaiian song
   c. Please wear Hawaiian clothes to the party because we are going to have a Hawaiian fashion contest. Be there!
   d. The Hawaiian clothes can be a Hawaiian shirt, a dress with a tropical print, or even sandals and a straw hat.

2

- Read the instructions for Step 2 aloud.
- Have students compare answers with a partner.
- Go over answers as a whole class.

7 Write! page 57

1

- Read the instructions for Steps 1 and 1a–b aloud, including the cues.
- Have students complete 1a–b individually.
- Walk around the classroom, helping students as necessary.

2

- Read the instructions for Step 2 aloud.
- Have students write their announcement and paragraph on lined paper or type it. Have them skip lines. Tell them you'll collect the paragraphs after they're revised in Parts 8 and 9.
- Have students complete Step 2 either at home or in class.

> **In your journal . . .** If time permits, read the journal entry instructions aloud. Tell students to write as many details about the party as they can. Students can write in class or at home.

8 Editing page 58

- Read the information box *So that and to* at the top of page 58.
- Call on a student to read the examples aloud.
- Point out that in sentences like these, *so that* is followed by a subject and a verb, whereas *to* is followed immediately by a verb.
- Point out that here, *so that* and *to* mean the same thing. Encourage students to use both forms in their writing to make it more interesting.

1

- Read the instructions for Step 1 aloud.
- Read sentences 1a–f aloud. Explain vocabulary as necessary.
- Have students work with a partner to complete 1a–f. They should discuss the answers together.
- Go over answers as a whole class.

Answers

1. a. I will go to the restaurant tomorrow so that I can make reservations for our party.
      I will go to the restaurant tomorrow to make reservations for our party.
   b. Let's swap lunches on Tuesday so that we can see what other people like to eat.
      Let's swap lunches on Tuesday to see what other people like to eat.
   c. I think we should go to the movie early so that we can buy popcorn and drinks for everyone.
      I think we should go to the movie early to buy popcorn and drinks for everyone.
   d. Let's meet at 6:15 so that we can get to the concert before it starts.
      Let's meet at 6:15 to get to the concert before it starts.
   e. Bring some money so that you can rent a boat at the lake.
      Bring some money to rent a boat at the lake.
   f. Please bring a hat so that you can keep from getting a sunburn.
      Please bring a hat to keep from getting a sunburn.

2

- Read the instructions for Step 2 aloud.
- Have students check their paragraphs from Part 7 in class or at home and revise as necessary.

- Have students share their revisions in groups, or have volunteers write their old and new sentences on the board.

9 Giving feedback page 59

Tell students that they are going to read each other's paragraphs and that they will need a sheet of paper for Step 2.

1

- Read the instructions for Steps 1 and 1a–b aloud.
- Have students exchange their paragraphs with a partner and complete 1a–b individually.
- Ask the class, *In 1b, how many people circled* fun? unique? Ask how many people wrote their own ideas to describe their partner's party, and what they were.
- Tell students to exchange books and review their partner's answers.

2

- Read the instructions for Step 2 aloud. Then call on a student to read the example letter.
- Have students write their letters to their partner individually.
- Walk around the classroom, helping students as necessary.

3

- Read the instructions for Step 3 aloud.
- Have students revise their paragraphs based on the comments they receive and other ideas they have. They can complete their revisions either in class or at home.
- Have students turn in their revised paragraphs to you.

4

- Read the instructions for Step 4 aloud.
- Give students time to walk around, look at the party ideas, and choose the ones they like best.
- Walk around the classroom with your students and make a list of the party ideas. Write the list on the board.

5

- Read the instructions for Step 5 aloud.
- Read the party ideas that you wrote on the board one at a time. Students raise their hands if they chose the idea as one of their three favorites. Tally the results to see which party is the class favorite.

> **Optional activity**
>
> **Party committees**
>
> If you are going to actually hold a class party, divide the class into committees. Each committee should be responsible for one aspect of the party as outlined in the party plans (e.g., food, music, clean up, etc.). Have them plan what they will do for the party and then present their plans to the rest of the class, who can point out anything they forgot. Then enjoy the party!

Just for fun page 60

Bring or ask students to bring materials such as markers or colored pencils, poster paper, magazines to cut up for pictures, stickers, scissors, glue, and tape to create a poster.

1

- Read the instructions for Steps 1 and 1a aloud.
- Read the words in the box aloud and have students repeat. Explain vocabulary as necessary.
- Read the instructions for 1b aloud, including the design ideas. Explain vocabulary as necessary.
- Have students complete 1a–b individually.

2

- Read the instructions for Step 2 aloud.
- Have students complete their posters individually.
- Walk around the classroom, helping students as necessary.
- If necessary, write these phrases on the board so groups can borrow materials from each other: *May I borrow the (tape)? Can I use the (blue marker)? Sure, go ahead. I'm sorry, I'm still using it.*
- Students can finish their posters at home, if necessary.

3

- Read the instructions for Step 3 aloud.
- Hang the posters around the room, and let students walk around to look at them and decide which parties they would like to attend. They do not need to choose the same parties they did in Part 9.

7 Thank-you note

Overview

In this unit, students write a thank-you letter to someone expressing appreciation. They also learn how to give reasons and use time markers such as *before*, *while*, and *after*.

In the prewriting activities, students learn different expressions to show their appreciation. They learn to support their points with specific examples and to put the events of a story in chronological order. The central writing assignment of the unit in Part 7 reviews the format for a letter. In the postwriting activity, students learn to shift clauses that begin with *after* and *before* to make their writing more interesting. The *Just for fun* activity shows students how to expand the skills they learned in the unit to write a thank-you card to someone in their school or neighborhood.

Key points

Students can sometimes become emotional when writing or listening to classmates' personal letters.

Encourage students to give their final thank-you letters to the people they wrote them to, and if possible, have them report on the recipients' reactions.

Students are introduced to basic elements related to narrative writing. Encourage students to relay important details so that their classmates can get a clear picture of the event they're describing.

Useful language for this unit includes expressions of thanks and appreciation; *Thank you for ____ing*; and *before*, *while*, and *after*.

Sections can be skipped. A minimal set of sections might include Parts 3, 4, 5, 6, and 7.

1 Brainstorming page 61

1

- Read the instructions for Step 1 aloud.
- Ask students to tell you what they see in the pictures. Provide vocabulary as necessary.
- Have a student read the examples aloud.
- Have students complete Step 1 individually.
- Go over responses with the whole class by reading each example aloud and having students raise their hands if they checked it.

2

- Read the instructions for Step 2 aloud.
- Have students complete Step 2 individually. Set a time limit of five minutes.
- Walk around the classroom, helping students as necessary. They may ask you for some new vocabulary words.

3

- Read the instructions for Step 3 aloud.
- Have students compare lists with a partner and add more ideas to their own lists.
- Call on some students to read their list of ideas aloud to the class or write them on the board.

> **Later in this unit . . .** Call on a student to read this aloud.

2 Analyzing a paragraph page 62

Ask students to brainstorm about gifts they've received. They can write a list on paper or just think.

1

- Read the instructions for Step 1 aloud. Have students read the paragraph individually.
- Call on students to read the paragraph aloud, sentence by sentence. Explain vocabulary as necessary.
- Read the instructions for a–d aloud.
- Have students complete a–d individually.
- Walk around the classroom, encouraging and helping students as necessary.
- If your students are having difficulty, you may want to stop after lb and review.
- Ask students to raise their hands or nod at you to let you know when they have finished.

2

- Have students compare answers with a partner.
- Go over answers as a whole class. Have students write the answers for lc–d on the board.

Talk about it. Read this aloud and have students talk with their partners for about five minutes.

Optional activity

Thank-you cards

Tell students that in English-speaking countries, it's customary for people to send thank-you cards after they've received birthday or holiday gifts. (If you have any samples, bring them to class.) Tell students that they are going to write a thank-you card for a gift they recently received. Have students work in groups and discuss gifts that they have recently received. They should say what the gift was and why they were thankful for it. They can use the language modeled in the paragraph on page 62. Then, using similar language, have them write thank-you cards. Suggest they send their cards to the gift givers.

3 Learning about organization page 63

- Read the information box *Giving reasons* at the top of page 63.
- Have students read the examples at the top of the page.

1

- Read the instructions for Steps 1 and 1a–d aloud. Explain vocabulary as necessary.
- Have students work with a partner to complete Step 1.
- Walk around the classroom, helping students as necessary.
- Go over answers as a whole class by calling on students to read the sentences aloud or write them on the board.

2

- Read the instructions for Step 2 aloud.
- Have students complete 2a–c individually.
- If some students are having difficulty, elicit examples from other students to demonstrate.
- Walk around the classroom, helping students as necessary.

3

- Read the instructions for Step 3 aloud.
- Call on a student to read the example in the illustration aloud.
- If possible, have students arrange their chairs in a circle so they can see everybody.
- Call on a student to start the chain.
- If you notice that not everyone is being thanked, encourage students to spontaneously make up a thank-you sentence for the students who have not been thanked yet, or create a sentence yourself thanking those students. Everyone should get a turn to thank and be thanked.

4 Working on content page 64

1

- Read the instructions for Step 1 aloud.
- Call on a student to read the examples aloud.

2

- Read the instructions for Step 2 aloud.
- Have students complete the chart individually.
- Walk around the classroom, helping students as necessary and checking their work.

3

- Read the instructions for Step 3 aloud.
- Give students several minutes to talk to their partners.
- Call on several students to share what their partners said with the class.

Optional activity

Extension of Step 3

Write the cues for Step 2 on the board, or ask students to memorize them. Have students close their books and stand up. When you say "Go," have students approach a classmate and ask the questions. Set a time limit of two minutes and then have them move on to another classmate. Continue the game for 10 to 12 minutes or until students are tired. Then ask the class: *What was the most surprising thing someone was thankful for? What was the nicest thing you heard?* If students get more ideas after Step 3, give them time to add them to their brainstorming lists from Part 1.

4

- Read the instructions for Step 4 aloud. Note that now they are switching from talking about someone in the third person *(he or she)* to the second person *(you)*.
- Have students complete Step 4 in class or at home.
- Walk around the classroom, helping students as necessary.
- Go over answers as a whole class or have students compare answers with a partner.

5 Learning more about organization
page 65

Read the information box *Time markers* at the top of page 65.

1

- Read the instructions for Step 1 aloud.
- Call on students to read 1a–c aloud.
- Have students compare answers with a partner.
- Go over the answers as a whole class.

Answer

1. b, a, c

2

- Read the instructions for Step 2 aloud.
- Read the paragraph aloud, skipping the blanks. Explain vocabulary as necessary.
- Have students complete Step 2 individually.
- Have students compare answers with a partner.
- Go over the answers as a whole class.

Answers

2. There is an old man I want to thank for giving me his jacket. One evening **after** school, I walked to the bus stop. **After** I got to the bus stop, it started to rain, but I did not have an umbrella. **While** I was waiting for the bus, I got wetter and wetter. About 10 minutes **before** the bus came, an old man walked up to the bus stop. He saw how wet I was, so he took off his jacket and gave it to me **while** we were talking. Even today, **after** so many years, I am still grateful to that man for his kindness.

3

- Read the instructions for Step 3 aloud.
- Have students complete 3a–c individually, either in class or at home.
- Have students compare sentences with a partner.
- Call on some students to write their sentences on the board. Walk around the classroom to check the other students' sentences.

6 Analyzing a model page 66
1

- Read the instructions for Step 1 aloud.
- Have students read the letter individually.
- Call on students to read the letter aloud, sentence by sentence. Explain vocabulary as necessary.
- Read the instructions for 1a–c aloud.
- Have students complete 1a–c individually.

Answers

1. a. Thank you so much for helping me at work yesterday.
   b. After; While; Then
   c. Let me thank you by taking you out to lunch sometime. I'm lucky to have a friend like you.

2

- Read the instructions for Step 2 aloud.
- Have students compare answers with a partner.
- Go over answers as a whole class.

7 Write! page 67

1

- Read the instructions for Steps 1 and 1a–d aloud.
- Have students complete Step 1 individually.
- Walk around the classroom, helping students as necessary.

2

- Read the instructions for Step 2 aloud.
- Have students write their letter on lined paper or type it. Have them skip lines. Tell them you'll collect the letters after they're revised in Parts 8 and 9.

> **In your journal . . .** If time permits, read the journal entry instructions aloud. Tell students they can also write about different ideas related to the nice thing they did. Ask them to use the time markers *before*, *while*, and *after* if they can. Students can write in class or at home.

8 Editing page 68

- Read the information box *Before, while, and after* at the top of page 68.
- Read the examples aloud. When you read the sentences that begin with *before* and *after*, pause after the first clause to show where the comma should go.

1

- Read the instructions for Step 1 aloud.
- Call on a student to read the first example aloud.
- Have students work with a partner to complete 1a–g. Remind students that they can use *before*, *while*, and *after* at the beginning of some sentences and in the middle of others. Remind them to use commas correctly.
- Students who finish early or higher-level students can write each item both ways (with *before*, *while*, or *after* at the beginning and in the middle).
- Go over answers as a whole class.

Answers

1. a. I was happy after I talked to you on the phone.
   b. I felt better after I got your advice.
   c. Before you lent me some money, I didn't know how generous you were.
   d. You listened to me while I was practicing my speech.
   e. I did not know how to solve my problem before I heard your advice.
   f. After you heard that I was in the hospital, you called me.
   g. While I was having trouble with my family, you called me every day and listened my problems.

2

- Read the instructions for Step 2 aloud.
- Have students who want to change the order of clauses in their paragraphs from Part 7 revise at home.
- Have students share their revisions in groups or have volunteers write their old and new sentences on the board.

9 Giving feedback page 69

Tell students that they are going to read each other's thank-you letter paragraphs and that they will need a sheet of paper for Step 2.

1

- Read the instructions for Steps 1 and 1a–b aloud.
- Have students exchange their paragraphs with a partner and complete 1a–b individually. Walk around the classroom, helping students as necessary.
- Tell students to exchange books and review their partner's answers.

2

- Read the instructions for Step 2 aloud. Then call on a student to read the example letter.
- Have students write their letters to their partner individually.
- Walk around the classroom, helping students as necessary.
- Have students give their letters to their partner. Give them time to tell their partner the answer to the question in the letter.

3

- Read the instructions for Step 3 aloud.

- Have students revise their paragraphs based on the comments they receive and other ideas they have. They can complete their revisions either in class or at home.

- Have students turn in their revised paragraphs to you.

Just for fun page 70

1

- Read the instructions for Step 1 aloud.

- Call on students to read the words in the box.

2

- Read the instructions for Step 2 aloud.

- Have students complete Step 2 individually.

- You may have to help students choose someone they'd like to thank. If necessary, have the class brainstorm some examples and write them on the board.

- Walk around and help students as necessary.

3

- Read the instructions for Step 3 aloud.

- Call on students to read the example letter.

- Have students complete their letters individually, either in class or at home. Have them type their letters if possible.

- Have students compare their letters in groups.

- If possible, check the letters for accuracy, and then have your students send them. Tell them to report back to the class if they get a response.

8 Movie review

Overview

In this unit, students write a review of a movie, including a summary and their opinion of the movie. They also learn how to write a two-paragraph composition.

In the prewriting activities, students write about the characters, actors, plot, and message of a movie. They support their opinion of the movie with details and examples. In Part 7, students organize their ideas into two paragraphs, with a topic sentence for each one. They end the second paragraph with a general conclusion. In the postwriting editing activity, students learn to avoid repetition of names by using pronouns. In the *Just for fun* activity, students work in groups to create a story for a movie, design a poster to advertise it, and hold a mock press conference.

Key points

From this unit on, students will write two paragraphs instead of one. More emphasis should be placed on teaching expository organization, such as putting different topics in separate paragraphs and clearly marking paragraph topics with topic sentences.

Guide students in their movie choices so that they do not all choose the same movies and so that they choose movies with plots and messages that are easy to write about.

You might have one or two students who rarely watch movies. Let them write book reviews instead.

Useful language for this unit includes present and past verb tenses, adjectives to describe movies, and pronouns.

Sections can be skipped. A minimal set of sections might include Parts 3, 4, 5, 6, and 7.

1 Brainstorming page 71

You might want to start this unit with a brief class discussion about movies. Ask students what kinds of movies they like.

1

- Read the instructions for Step 1 aloud.
- Ask students to tell you what they see in the pictures. Provide vocabulary as necessary.

- Read the movie titles in 1a–f aloud and have students repeat.
- Have students work with a partner to complete 1a–f.
- Have students check their answers at the right side of the page.
- Ask the class, *How many people have seen* Toy Story*?* The Lord of the Rings*?* etc., and have students raise their hands. Call on a few students to give their opinions of the movies.

Answers
1. a. 3
   b. 1
   c. 6
   d. 2
   e. 5
   f. 4

2

- Read the instructions for Step 2 aloud.
- Note: Explain to students that *italics*, a style of writing that slants to the right, is used to denote movie titles in printed material. Tell them that underlining represents italics in handwritten form.
- Have students complete Step 2 individually. Set a time limit of five minutes.
- Walk around the classroom, helping students as necessary. They may ask you for some new vocabulary words related to titles. They may also write movie titles in their own language, if necessary.

3

- Read the instructions for Step 3 aloud.
- Have students compare lists with a partner and add more ideas to their own lists.
- Call on some students to read their lists of ideas aloud to the class or write them on the board.

Later in this unit . . . Call on a student to read this aloud.

2 Analyzing a paragraph page 72

1

- Read the instructions for Step 1 aloud.
- Have students read the paragraph individually. Explain vocabulary as necessary.
- Call on students to read the paragraph aloud, sentence by sentence.
- Read the instructions for 1a–d aloud.
- Have students answer 1a–d individually.
- If your students are having a difficult time, you may want to stop after lb and review.
- Ask students to raise their hands or nod at you to let you know when they have finished.

2

- Have students compare answers with a partner.
- Go over answers as a whole class. If any students have seen the movies mentioned, ask them if they agree with the main message.

> **Answers**
>
> 1. a. Characters: Jake, Neytiri; Actors: Sam Worthington, Zoe Saldana
>   b. we must try to understand other cultures
>   c. *Toy Story 3* is a movie about what happens to toys when their owner grows up.
>   d. The main message of *Toy Story 3* is that we can solve problems if we work together.

> **Talk about it.**   Read this aloud and have students talk with their partners for about five minutes.

3 Learning about organization page 73

- Tell students that movie summaries, like the ones they will write, give readers the most important information about a movie.
- Read the information box *Movie summary* at the top of page 73.
- Write the following on the board: *the characters and actors*; *the plot*; *the message*.
- Elicit definitions from the students and write them on the board: *the characters and actors – people in a movie, stars of a movie*; *the plot – what happens in the movie, the story*; *the message – what the movie is trying to tell or teach the audience*.

1

- Read the instructions for Step 1 aloud.
- Give students a minute or so to choose a movie and write it down.
- You may want to ask students to share what movies they've chosen.

2

- Read the instructions for Step 2 aloud.
- Have students read the parts of the three movie summaries individually.
- Call on students to read the parts of the three movie summaries aloud. Explain vocabulary as necessary.
- Read the instructions for 2a–c aloud.
- Have students complete 2a–c individually.
- Have students compare responses with a partner. Walk around while students are talking to check their work.

> ***Optional activity***
>
> **The sequel**
>
> Ask students if they know what a sequel is. If not, explain that it is a movie that is a continuation of a first movie. Give some examples (e.g., the *Star Wars* movies, the *Harry Potter* movies, the *Matrix* movies). Have students work in small groups. Each group should pick a movie that doesn't already have a sequel. They should discuss an idea for a sequel and then write a summary of the sequel, including the information modeled in Part 3. When they are finished, have them present their summaries to the class.

4 Learning more about organization
page 74

- Ask students how they decide whether or not they will go to a movie. Elicit answers (e.g., from advertisements, from a friend's recommendation, because popular stars are in it). Tell them that many people decide to see a movie based on a movie review, which is what they will read and write in this unit.
- Read the information box *Movie opinion* at the top of page 74. Explain vocabulary as necessary.

1

- Read the instructions for Step 1 aloud.
- Have students read the paragraph individually.
- Call on students to read the paragraph aloud, sentence by sentence. Explain vocabulary as necessary.
- Tell students that the second paragraph begins when the main topic changes.
- Have students complete Step 1 individually.
- Go over answers with the whole class. Ask students to tell you the topic of the first paragraph (summary of the movie) and the second paragraph (the writer's opinion of the movie).

Answer

1. *Bend It Like Beckham* was very entertaining.

2

- Read the instructions for Step 2 aloud.
- Have students work with a partner to complete 2a–d.
- Go over answers as a whole class.
- Ask if any students have seen this movie. If they have, elicit their opinions about it.

Answers

2. a. 1
   b. 2
   c. 2
   d. 1

3

- Read the instructions for Step 3 and the words in the box aloud. Explain vocabulary as necessary.
- Have students complete Step 3 individually.
- Walk around the classroom, helping students as necessary. They may ask you for some vocabulary.
- Have students compare answers with a partner or in small groups.
- Ask who wrote their own words. Write the new words on the board for the whole class.

5 Working on content page 75

1

- Read the instructions for Step 1 aloud.
- Read the instructions for 1a–b aloud, including the questions. Have students suggest additional questions and write them on the board.
- Have students work with a partner to complete 1a–b.
- Walk around the classroom, helping students as necessary.

2

- Read the instructions for Step 2 aloud.
- Have a student read the example aloud. Point out that the last sentence contains the recommendation.
- Have students complete Step 2 individually
- Have students compare responses with a partner. Walk around the classroom, helping students as necessary and checking their work.

Optional activity

Talk show: Movie review

Have students work with a partner to practice a talk show in which they review a movie. Each student gives his or her opinion of the movie, supported by reasons. The students do not have to agree with each other. Have them create a rating system for each movie (one to four stars, or a thumb up / thumb down). Give each pair a few minutes to present their talk show to the class.

6 Analyzing a model page 76

1

- Read the instructions for Step 1 aloud.
- Have students read the paragraphs individually.
- Call on students to read the paragraphs aloud. Explain vocabulary as necessary.
- Read the instructions for 1a–d aloud.
- Have students complete 1a–d individually or with a partner.

1. a. *Slumdog Millionaire* is a movie about a poor boy who gets rich on a TV show; I think *Slumdog Millionaire* is a great movie.

   b. 1. Dev Patel, Freida Pinto   2. People from the slums have hard lives, but they can still do great things, especially when they trust their love.   3. I think *Slumdog Millionaire* is a great movie.   4. I think everyone should see this wonderful movie.

   c. saw, liked; because Jun saw the movie before writing this review

   d. Anyone can succeed if they try.

2

- Read the instructions for Step 2 aloud.
- Have students compare answers with a partner.
- Go over answers as a whole class.

7 Write! page 77

1

- Read the instructions for Steps 1 and 1a–b aloud.
- Have students work individually to fill in their charts.
- Walk around and help students as necessary.

2

- Read the instructions for Step 2 aloud.
- Have students write their paragraphs on lined paper or type them. Have them skip lines. Tell them you'll collect the paragraphs after they're revised in Parts 8 and 9.

> **In your journal . . .** If time permits, read the journal entry instructions aloud. Tell students they can also write about their favorite and least favorite actors. Students can write in class or at home.

8 Editing page 78

- Read the information box *Pronouns* at the top of page 78. Explain vocabulary as necessary.
- Call on students to read the examples aloud.
- Explain that students should avoid repeating names too much because it becomes boring.

- Students do not need to learn the names of the different types of pronouns.

1

- Read the instructions for Step 1 aloud.
- Have students complete Step 1 individually. Point out that Harry and Ron are boys and that Hermione is a girl.
- If students are having difficulty, tell them there are 12 changes to be made.
- Have students compare answers with a partner.
- Go over answers as a whole class. Point out that not every name can be replaced by a pronoun because then the text would be confusing.

1.   One message of the *Harry Potter* movies is that good friends are important. Harry has many problems in his life. He is always in danger. However, Harry solves his problems because he has some good friends to help him. The good friends are not typical kids. The good friends know magic and have some special skills. Harry's best friend is Ron. He is loyal and dependable. He often helps Harry get out of danger. Harry's other good friend is Hermione. She is very smart and good at her studies. Hermione helps Harry with his homework. Harry depends a lot on Ron and Hermione, and they help him through many adventures. Their friendship is one of my favorite things about the movies.

2

- Read the instructions for Step 2 aloud.
- Have students who want to change names to pronouns in their paragraphs from Part 7 revise them at home.
- Have students share their revisions in groups or have volunteers write their old and new sentences on the board.

9 Giving feedback page 79

Tell students that they are going to read one another's reviews and that they'll need a sheet of paper for 1c.

1

- Read the instructions for Steps 1 and 1a–c aloud.
- Have students sit with their groups and take turns reading another group's reviews.

- Have students complete 1a–b with their groups.
- Walk around the classroom, helping students as necessary.
- Tell students to exchange books and review their partner's answers.
- Read the instructions for 1c aloud. Then call on a student to read the example letter.
- Have students write their letters to their partner individually.
- Walk around the classroom, helping students as necessary.
- Have students give their letters to their partner. Give them time to tell their partner the answer to the question in the letter.

2

- Read the instructions for Step 2 aloud.
- Have students revise their paragraphs based on the comments they receive and other ideas they have. They can complete their revisions either in class or at home.
- Have students turn in their revised paragraphs to you.

Just for fun page 80

Students will need large pieces of paper or poster board and colored pencils or markers.

1

- Read the instructions for Step 1 aloud.
- Have students work in groups to decide on a movie name. Set a time limit of three to five minutes.

2

- Read the instructions for Step 2 aloud.
- Students can discuss their ideas and have one person write them down, or write their ideas individually and then discuss them. Set a time limit of 15 minutes.

3

- Read the instructions for Step 3 aloud.
- Have students work in their groups to complete Step 3. Have them use the names of real actors.

4

- Read the instructions for Step 4 and the example movie poster aloud. Point out that the poster shows the movie title, the actors, the characters, and the plot.
- Have students work in their groups to complete Step 4.
- Walk around the classroom, helping students as necessary.

5

- Read the instructions for Steps 5 and 5a–b aloud.
- Have students complete 5a–b with the same group they worked with in Steps 1–4. Encourage students to be dramatic and have fun.
- If time permits, have each group present their press conference and poster to the class.
- Display the posters around the classroom.

9 *Friendship*

Overview

In this unit, students write about a friend. They also learn to write supporting sentences.

In the prewriting activities, students learn vocabulary for describing people and brainstorm qualities of a good friend. They strengthen their opinions by writing supporting sentences that give examples. In Part 7, students write two paragraphs about their friend. In the first paragraph, they describe the qualities that make the person a good friend. In the second paragraph, they write about something they would like to do for their friend. In the postwriting editing activity, students learn to connect result clauses with a main sentence by using *so*. In the *Just for fun* activity, students interview a classmate and write a magazine article based on the interesting information they discover.

Key points

Encourage students to choose a friend that has admirable personal qualities that they can support with examples. The friend could also be a family member.

The final task in this unit could be to give the paragraphs to the person written about, which you might want to explain early in the unit. If possible, have students report on the recipients' reactions.

Useful language includes vocabulary to describe people and personalities; *will* and *would like*; and *so* to connect sentences.

Sections can be skipped. A minimal set of sections might include Parts 4, 5, 6, and 7

1 Brainstorming page 81

1

- Read the instructions for Step 1 aloud. Tell students that for now, they should think about friends in general, not a specific person.
- Read the words in the box and have the class repeat. Then read sentences 1a–f, skipping the blanks. Explain vocabulary as necessary.
- Have students work with a partner to complete 1a–f.
- Go over answers as a whole class.

Answers
1. a. kind
   b. funny
   c. dependable
   d. honest
   e. generous
   f. loyal

2

- Read the instructions for Step 2 aloud. Tell students they should now think of specific people.
- Have students complete Step 2 individually. Set a time limit of five minutes.
- Walk around the classroom, helping students as necessary.

3

- Read the instructions for Step 3 aloud.
- Have students compare lists with a partner and add more ideas to their own lists.
- Call on some students to read their lists of ideas aloud to the class or write them on the board.

> **Later in this unit . . .** Call on a student to read this aloud.

2 Analyzing a paragraph page 82

1

- Read the instructions for Step 1 aloud.
- Have students read the paragraph individually.
- Call on students to read the paragraph aloud, sentence by sentence. Explain vocabulary as necessary.
- Read the instructions for 1a–d aloud.
- Have students complete 1a–d individually.
- If students are having difficulty, you may want to stop after lb and review.
- Ask students to raise their hands or nod at you to let you know when they have finished.

2

- Have students compare answers with a partner.
- Go over answers as a whole class.
- Have students write the answers to lc–d on the board.

Answers

1. a. dependable, honest, funny
   b. She is there whenever I need someone to talk to, and she always tells me the truth. If I am sad, Lisa makes me feel better with her jokes.
   c. Josh is my best friend.
   d. Josh is cheerful, generous, and friendly.

Talk about it.   Read this aloud and have students talk with their partners for about five minutes.

Optional activity

A friend is someone who is . . .

Have students work individually to complete this sentence with one or two adjectives. They can look up words in their dictionaries or ask you for help. Have students write their sentences on the board. How many students chose the same qualities?

---

3 Working on content   page 83

1

- Read the instructions for Step 1 aloud.
- Call on students to read each of the sentences in the Friendship Chart aloud. Explain vocabulary as necessary.
- Have students complete the chart individually. Point out that the answers are the students' own opinions. There are no "right" answers.
- Go over responses as a whole class by reading each sentence aloud and asking, *How many people ranked this as very important? Not so important?* Have students raise their hands to show their responses.

2

- Read the instructions for Step 2 aloud.
- Have students complete Step 2 individually.

- Walk around the classroom, helping students as necessary.
- Have students compare answers with a partner or group.

---

4 Learning about organization   page 84

- Read the information box *Supporting sentences* at the top of page 84.
- Call on a student to read the examples aloud.
- Point out that supporting sentences make statements easier to understand by giving more specific information.

1

- Read the instructions for Step 1 aloud. Point out that these sentences are not about the person they chose in Part 3, Step 2.
- Have students complete Step 1 individually.
- Have students compare their responses with a partner or a group.

2

- Read the instructions for Step 2 aloud. Point out that these sentences are about the person they chose in Part 3.
- Have students complete Step 2 individually.
- Walk around the classroom, helping students as necessary.
- Go over responses as a whole class. Call on students to read their sentences aloud or write them on the board.

Optional activity

Additional support

Write several of the adjectives from Parts 1 and 3 on the board. Have students work with a partner. Assign the same one or two adjectives to two pairs. Tell them to write three or more supporting sentences to explain the adjective(s). Then have the pairs compare their sentences.

5 Working more on content page 85

1

- Read the instructions for Step 1 aloud.
- Call on students to read the examples in the pictures.
- Have students complete Step 1 individually.
- Go over responses as a whole class by asking students to read their responses aloud.

2

- Read the instructions for Step 2 aloud.
- Call on a student to read the example aloud. Explain vocabulary as necessary.
- Have students complete Step 2 individually. Encourage them to make plans that they could realistically carry out.
- Walk around the classroom, helping students as necessary.

3

- Have students compare their charts with a partner.
- Tell students that they may make additions to their original chart.

6 Analyzing a model page 86

1

- Read the instructions for Step 1 aloud.
- Have students read the paragraphs individually.
- Call on students to read the paragraphs aloud. Explain vocabulary as necessary.
- Read the instructions for 1a–e aloud. Point out that before students underline the topic sentence in 1a, they should determine what the topic of the paragraph is.
- Have students complete 1a–e.

Answers

1. a. Carla, one of my best friends, is honest, dependable, and trustworthy.
   b. honest, dependable, trustworthy
   c. she always tells me the truth about everything – even about how I look
      she always does what she says she is going to do
      She never tells anyone the secrets I tell her.
   d. I think it will be a lonely time for her, so I would like to invite her to come and stay at my house with my family.
   e. Carla, My Friend; Taking a Friend to My Home

2

- Have students compare answers with a partner.
- Go over answers as a whole class.

7 Write! page 87

1

- Read the instructions for Step 1 aloud.
- Call on students to read the information about the contents of the two paragraphs aloud.

2

- Read the instructions for Steps 2 and 2a–d aloud.
- Have students write their titles. Walk around and help students as necessary.

Answers

2. a. I Have a Friend Whose Name Is Charlie
   b. Introducing Joan to a Friend in Vietnam
   c. A New Friend I Made
   d. (Answers will vary.)

3

- Read the instructions for Step 3 aloud.
- Have students write their two paragraphs on lined paper or type them. Have them skip lines. Tell them you'll collect the paragraphs after they're revised in Parts 8 and 9.

In your journal . . . If time permits, read the journal entry instructions aloud. Tell students that they can also write about the kind of friend they would like to be using the structure *would like* to explain their ideas. Students can write in class or at home.

8 Editing page 88

- Read the information box *Combining sentences with so* at the top of page 88.
- Call on a student to read the examples aloud. Point out that a comma precedes the clause that begins with *so*.
- Ask students to look back at the second paragraph in Part 6, Step 1, and underline the sentence connected with *so*. (Answer: I think it will be a lonely time for her, so I would like to invite her to come and stay at my house with my family.)

1

- Read the instructions for Step 1 aloud.
- Call on a student to read 1a aloud.
- Have students work with a partner to complete Step 1. Make sure they identify the result before writing the new sentence.
- Walk around the classroom, helping students as necessary.
- Go over answers as a whole class.

Answers

1. a. Naoki loves soccer, so I want to take him to a soccer game.
   b. Cristina never tells secrets, so I know I can trust her.
   c. I have known Eduardo since we were six, so he knows a lot about me.
   d. My best friend moved away, so I am lonely.
   e. Ryan needs to buy a new car, so I will lend him some money.
   f. Sara loves computer games, so I will buy her some new software.

2

- Read the instructions for Step 2 aloud.
- Have students who want to combine sentences revise their paragraphs from Part 7 at home.
- Have students share their revisions in groups, or have volunteers write their old and new sentences on the board.

9 Giving feedback page 89

Tell students that they are going to read each other's paragraphs and that they will need a sheet of paper for Step 2.

1

- Read the instructions for Steps 1 and 1a–d aloud.
- Have students exchange their paragraphs with a partner and complete 1a–d individually. Walk around the classroom, helping students as necessary.
- When they finish, ask the class, *In 1c, how many people circled (fun)?* See which was the most popular adjective chosen. Ask how many people wrote their own ideas and what they were.
- Tell students to exchange books and review their partner's answers.

2

- Read the instructions for Step 2 aloud. Then call on a student to read the example letter.
- Have students write their letters to their partner individually.
- Walk around the classroom, helping students as necessary.
- Have students turn in their revised paragraphs to you.

3

- Read the instructions for Step 3 aloud.
- Have students give their letters to their partner. Give them time to tell their partner the answer to the question in the letter.
- Have students revise their paragraphs based on the comments they receive and other ideas they have. They can complete their revisions either in class or at home.

Just for fun page 90

Ask students if they've ever read magazine articles about people. Ask: *Where have you read these articles? What makes them interesting?*

1

- Read the instructions for Step 1 aloud.
- Ask students to tell you what they see in the picture. Provide vocabulary as necessary.
- Have students read the paragraph individually.
- Call on students to read the paragraph aloud, sentence by sentence. Explain vocabulary as necessary.

2

- Read the instructions for Step 2 and the words from the box aloud.
- Have the class brainstorm some examples of questions on each topic and write them on the board.
- Have students work with a partner to interview each other. Set a time limit of seven to ten minutes.
- Walk around the classroom, helping students as necessary.

3

- Read the instructions for Step 3 aloud.
- Have students complete Step 3 individually.

4

- Read the instructions for Step 4 aloud.
- Have students complete their articles individually, in class or at home.
- Have students exchange their articles with their partner. Give them time to discuss the articles and make changes, if necessary.
- Walk around the classroom, helping students as necessary and checking their work.

5

- Read the instructions for Step 5 aloud.
- Call on students to give some possible titles for their articles.
- You may wish to have students type (that would be ideal) or write their articles neatly so you can put them into a class magazine.

6

- Read the instructions for Step 6 aloud.
- Have students take a photo (or draw a picture) of their classmate.
- If possible, compile everyone's articles and photos and put a magazine together for the class. Students can then sign it or write special messages by their pictures or on the covers.

10 *Superhero powers*

Overview

In this unit, students write about a superhero power they would like to have, such as the ability to travel through time. They also learn how to write about situations that are not real.

In the prewriting activities, students make wishes about superhero powers they would like to have and discuss with classmates what those wishes might mean. They learn to logically connect problems with imaginary solutions. In Part 7, they write one paragraph about a specific problem they have and a superhero power that would solve it and a second paragraph about what they would do with that power. In the postwriting editing activity, they practice structures for expressing wishes. The *Just for fun* activity lets students work with a partner to create a comic strip, combining art with their writing.

Key points

This unit brings out students' imaginations and creativity. Brainstorm some popular superheroes with your class to set the mood. Bring to class examples of comic books or short video clips, if possible.

Make sure students come up with a specific problem the superpower would allow them to solve. They do not need to choose a significant or deeply personal problem. Students can choose an ordinary situation such as not wanting to ride a crowded bus, which could be solved by being able to fly.

Useful language for this unit includes *I wish I could . . .* , *If I could . . .* , *I would . . .* , and *If I were . . .*

Sections can be skipped. A minimal set of sections might include Parts 3, 4, 5, 6, and 7.

1 Brainstorming page 91

1

■ Read the instructions for Step 1 and the phrases in the box aloud. Explain vocabulary as necessary.

■ Ask students to tell you what they see in the pictures. Provide vocabulary if necessary.

■ Have students work with a partner to complete Step 1.

■ Go over answers with the whole class.

■ Ask students if they know of a superhero that can do any of the things mentioned in the box.

Answers

1. a. see through walls
   b. travel through time
   c. become invisible
   d. fly
   e. breathe underwater
   f. read minds

2

■ Read the instructions for Step 2 aloud.

■ Have students complete Step 2 individually. Set a time limit of five minutes.

■ Walk around the classroom, helping students as necessary.

3

■ Read the instructions for Step 3 aloud.

■ Have students compare lists with a partner and add more ideas to their own lists.

■ Call on some students to read their list of ideas aloud to the class or write them on the board.

> **Later in this unit . . .** Call on a student to read this aloud.

Optional activity

Who's your favorite superhero? What can he or she do?

Have students work alone to write about their favorite superhero (now or when they were a child) and what the superhero can do. After five minutes, have students work in groups and share their information. If time permits, call on students one at a time to name their favorite superheroes. Write the names on the board. Who is the class favorite? What can he or she do?

2 Analyzing a paragraph page 92

1

- Read the instructions for Step 1 aloud.
- Ask students to tell you what they see in the picture. Provide vocabulary as necessary.
- Have students read the paragraph individually.
- Call on students to read the paragraph aloud, sentence by sentence.
- Read the instructions for 1a–d aloud.
- Have students answer 1a–d individually.
- If your students are having a difficult time, you may want to stop after 1b and review.
- Ask students to raise their hands or nod at you to let you know when they have finished.

2

- Have students compare answers with a partner.
- Go over answers as a whole class. Call on students to write the answers to 1c–d on the board. Check punctuation.

Answers

1. a. I am often late for work because of traffic jams.
   b. explains how to solve a problem
   c. I wish I could see the future.
   d. If I could see the future, I would be able to get rich.

Talk about it. Read this aloud and have students talk with their partners for about five minutes.

3 Working on content page 93

1

- Read the instructions for Step 1 aloud.
- Call on students to read the superhero powers in the box aloud. Explain vocabulary as necessary.

2

- Read the instructions for Step 2 aloud.
- Have students complete Step 2 individually.
- Walk around the classroom, helping students as necessary.
- Go over answers as a whole class.

3

- Read the instructions for Step 3 aloud. Tell students that they will be taking a kind of psychology test to see what their wishes mean.
- Have students complete Step 3 individually.
- Walk around the classroom, helping students as necessary. Explain vocabulary as necessary.

Answers will vary. Possible answers:

3. a. 3
   b. 4
   c. 5
   d. 6
   e. 2
   f. 1

4

- Read the instructions for Step 4 aloud.
- Call on two students to read the example conversation aloud.
- Have students work with a partner to complete Step 4.
- Go over responses as a whole class. You might want to make a class chart to find out which was the most popular superhero power. Ask students if they thought their partner's interpretation was correct.

4 Working more on content page 94

1

- Read the instructions for Step 1 aloud.
- Call on a student to read the thought bubbles aloud.
- Have students complete Step 1 with a partner.
- Go over answers as a whole class.

Answers

1. a. 2
   b. 3
   c. 1
   d. 1
   e. 2
   f. 3

2

- Read the instructions for Step 2 aloud.
- Call on a student to read the examples aloud.
- Have students complete Step 2 individually.
- Walk around the classroom, helping students as necessary.

3

- Read the instructions for Step 3 aloud.
- Have students complete Step 3 with their partner.
- Go over responses as a whole class. Call on some students to tell the class what powers they chose and what problems they can solve.

5 Learning about organization page 95

- Read the information box *Adding examples to a wish* at the top of page 95.
- Have a student read the example sentences aloud.
- Point out the placement of the comma after *If I could* . . . .
- Ask students how many of them would like to communicate with their pets or other animals.

1

- Read the instructions for Step 1 aloud.
- Have students complete 1a–d individually.
- Go over answers as a whole class. Call on students to write the sentences on the board. Check punctuation.

Answers

1. a. If I could talk to animals, I would ask Ginger why she likes to chew on my shoes.
   b. If I could talk to animals, I would ask her / Ginger why she's afraid of the vacuum cleaner.
   c. If I could talk to animals, I would ask her / Ginger how she feels about mice.
   d. If I could talk to animals, I would teach her / Ginger how to use the TV.

2

- Read the instructions for Step 2 aloud.
- Have students complete Step 2 individually. Point out that they are writing notes, not complete sentences.
- Walk around the classroom, helping students as necessary. They may ask you for some vocabulary.

3

- Read the instructions for Step 3 aloud.
- Have students complete Step 3 individually.
- Have students compare answers with a partner.
- Go over answers as a whole class. Write or have students write several examples on the board.

Optional activity

If you could see the future

Tell students that they have been granted the power to see the future, but that they can only do *one* thing with this special power. Give students a few minutes to write sentences about what thing they will choose to see and why. Then have students stand up and share their sentences with as many other students as possible in 10 minutes. After time is up, ask students about the choices they heard from their classmates. This game can also be played by asking students to pretend they could change one event in the past.

6 Analyzing a model page 96

1

- Read the instructions for Step 1 aloud.
- Have students read the paragraphs individually.
- Call on students to read the paragraphs aloud, sentence by sentence. Explain vocabulary as necessary.
- Read the instructions for 1a–c aloud.
- Have students complete 1a–c individually.

2

- Read the instructions for Step 2 aloud.
- Have students compare answers with a partner.
- Go over answers as a whole class.

7 Write! page 97

1

- Read the instructions for Steps 1 and 1a–b, including the cues that follow, aloud.
- Have students complete 1a–b individually.
- Walk around the classroom, helping students as necessary.

2

- Read the instructions for Step 2 aloud.
- Have students complete Step 2 individually.

3

- Have students write their paragraphs on lined paper or type them. Have them skip lines.
- Tell them you'll collect the paragraphs after they're revised in Parts 8 and 9.

> **In your journal . . .** If time permits, read the journal entry instructions aloud. Tell students that they can also write about their current favorite superhero or fictional character. Students can write in class or at home.

8 Editing page 98

- Read the information box *Writing about wishes* at the top of page 98.
- Call on students to read the examples aloud.
- Point out that these are all different ways to express wishes. Point out the structure *I wish I were*. Tell students that people sometimes say *I wish I was*, but they use the more traditional *I wish I were* in writing. Point out that when we're expressing wishes or desires, *want* will usually be followed by *to*.
- Ask students to look at the paragraphs in Part 6, Step 1, and underline any sentences with *want to* or *wish*. (Answer: I want to be able to communicate more with Ginger, so I wish I could talk to animals.) Ask them to notice how every sentence in paragraph 2 uses *If I / we could . . .* or *I / we would . . . .*

1

- Read the instructions for Step 1 aloud. Explain that in some cultures, people write their wishes on slips of paper and tie them to the branches of a tree.
- Have students complete 1a–f individually.
- Have students compare answers with a partner.
- Go over answers as a whole class.

2

- Read the instructions for Step 2 aloud.
- Have students check their paragraphs from Part 7 in class or at home and revise as necessary.
- Have students share their revisions in groups, or have volunteers write their old and new sentences on the board.

9 Giving feedback page 99

Tell students that they are going to read each other's paragraphs and that they will need a sheet of paper for Step 2.

1

- Read the instructions for Steps 1 and 1a aloud.
- Have students exchange their paragraphs with a classmate and complete 1a individually.
- Read the instructions for 1b–c aloud.
- Have students work in groups of four. The people they exchanged paragraphs with should not be in their groups.
- Have students take turns telling the group about the paragraphs they read.
- Have students complete 1b–c in their groups. Walk around the classroom, helping students as necessary.
- When they finish, ask the class, *In 1b, what was the best superhero power you chose?* Also see which was the most unusual, funniest, and most practical superhero power chosen. Ask how many people wrote their own ideas and what they were.

2

- Read the instructions for Step 2 aloud.
- Call on a student to read the example letter aloud.
- Have students write their letters to their partner from 1a individually.
- Walk around the classroom, helping students as necessary.
- Have students give their letters to their partner. Give them time to tell their partner the answer to the question in the letter.

3

- Read the instructions for Step 3 aloud.
- Have students revise their paragraphs based on the comments they receive and other ideas they have. They can complete their revisions either in class or at home.
- Have students turn in their revised paragraphs to you.

Just for fun page 100

- Bring or have students bring markers or colored pencils to class.
- Students can also write and design their comic on a computer, if they wish.
- Ask the class to tell you what comic books they know. If any students are current comic book fans, let the rest of the class ask them some questions about their interests.

1

- Read the instructions for Steps 1 and 1a–c aloud.
- Have a student read the sample comic aloud. Explain vocabulary as necessary.
- Have students complete 1a–c with a partner.
- Have students discuss their ideas with a partner.

2

- Read the instructions for Step 2 aloud.
- Call on students to read the example story notes.
- Have students work with their partner to complete Step 2. They should discuss their ideas, choose a story together, and then write notes.

3

- Read the instructions for Step 3 aloud.
- Call on students to read the comic captions and dialog aloud.
- Have students complete Step 3 with their partner. They can take turns writing and drawing, or one student can write and the other one draw.
- If some students want to draw very detailed comics, have them complete their work at home.
- Display all the comics on a large table or post them around the room so everyone can read them.

11 Advertisements

Overview

In this unit, students write a magazine advertisement for a product. They also learn how to use advertising language.

In the prewriting activities, students write claims about what a product can do. They learn techniques for catching the reader's attention in the first few lines of a paragraph, and they learn how to end the paragraph with a recommendation to the buyer. In Part 7, students write a one-paragraph testimonial from someone who has used the product and a second paragraph describing what the product is and what it can do. In the postwriting editing activity, students practice using superlatives to describe their products. The *Just for fun* activity has students recycle the advertising language they practiced as they set up a class market.

Key points

Try to begin the unit with a TV or Internet commercial or a magazine advertisement to help set the scene. Make sure the advertisement has a user testimonial.

Tell students whether they should write advertisements about realistic or fanciful products (such as "self-folding clothes"). Parts 1–3 display realistic products, and Parts 4–7 focus on fanciful products.

To focus on real-world applications, you can have your students write advertisements for products related to their field of work or interest. Students might also write advertisements for local merchants.

Useful language for this unit includes imperatives and superlative adjectives.

Sections can be skipped. A minimal set of sections might include Parts 3, 4, 5, 6, and 7.

1 Brainstorming page 101

Ask students where they see advertisements (on the Internet, in magazines, on billboards, in subways, etc.). Ask them what their favorite advertisements are.

1

- Read the instructions for Step 1 aloud.
- Ask students to tell you what they see in the pictures. Provide vocabulary as necessary.

- Call on students to read the advertising claims aloud.
- Have students complete 1a–d with a partner.
- Go over answers as a whole class.

> **Answers**
> 1. a. 3
>   b. 1
>   c. 4
>   d. 2

2

- Read the instructions for Step 2 aloud.
- Have students complete Step 2 individually. Set a time limit of five minutes.
- Walk around the classroom, helping students as necessary. They may ask you for some new vocabulary words.

3

- Read the instructions for Step 3 aloud.
- Have students compare lists with a partner and add more ideas to their own lists.
- Call on some students to read their list of ideas aloud to the class or write them on the board.

> **Later in this unit . . .** Call on a student to read this aloud.

2 Analyzing a paragraph page 102

1

- Read the instructions for Steps 1 and 1a–d aloud.
- Ask students to tell you what they see in the picture.
- Have students read the paragraph individually.
- Call on students to read the paragraph aloud, sentence by sentence. Explain vocabulary as necessary
- Have students complete 1a–d individually.
- If your students are having a difficult time, you may want to stop after 1b and review.
- Ask students to raise their hands or nod at you to let you know when they have finished.

2

- Have students compare answers with a partner
- Go over answers as a whole class. Have students write the answers for lc–d on the board.

Talk about it. Read this aloud and have students talk with their partners for about five minutes.

Optional activity

Analyzing real advertisements

Bring in or have students bring in advertisements from newspapers or magazines. Have students work in groups, and give each group several advertisements to look at. They should go over each advertisement, choose a favorite, and write a short description telling what the product is and what it does. Collect the descriptions and the advertisements. Post the advertisements around the room and read the descriptions aloud. Have the class point to the one that is being described.

3 Working on content page 103

Write the words *advertising claim* and *advertising recommendation* on the board and ask students if they know what the words mean.

1

- Read the instructions for Step 1 and the Word File aloud.
- Read sentences 1a–d aloud. Explain vocabulary as necessary.
- Have students work with a partner to complete 1a–d.
- Walk around the classroom, helping students as necessary.
- Go over answers as a whole class. Have students write the answers on the board.

2

- Read the instructions for Step 2 and the example aloud.
- Point out the comma after the *if* clause.
- Have students complete 2a–d individually.
- Walk around the classroom, helping students as necessary.
- Elicit responses from the class and write some examples on the board.

3

- Read the instructions for Step 3 aloud.
- Call on students to read the headings in the box and the examples aloud.
- Have students complete Step 3 individually.
- Go over answers as a whole class.

4 Learning about organization page 104

- Read the information box *Attention getters* at the top of page 104.
- Call on a student to read the examples of attention getters aloud.

1

- Read the instructions for Step 1 aloud.
- Ask students to tell you what they see in the pictures. Provide vocabulary as necessary.
- Have students complete 1a–d individually.

- Go over answers as a whole class.
- Ask the class: *Which attention getters are sentences?* (Answers: a and d) *Which attention getter is a question?* (Answer: c) *Which are surprising or funny?* (Answers: a, c, and d) *Which are about problems people have?* (Answers: b and c)

> **Answers**
>
> 1. a. 2
>   b. 1
>   c. 4
>   d. 3

2

- Read the instructions for Step 2 aloud.
- Encourage students by telling them that the drawing doesn't have to be "professional"! Remind them to have fun with it.
- Have students write their attention getters.
- Have students compare with a partner.

> **Optional activity**
>
> **Advertising agency**
>
> Tell students that when an advertising agency launches a new product, they work in teams to think of clever ways to get people's attention. Bring to class about five different products, such as a toothbrush, sunglasses, a cell phone, or an article of clothing. Have students work in small groups to choose a few products and write attention getters. When they finish, have groups share their ideas with the class. Give students time to change the attention getter they wrote in Part 4, Step 2, if they would like.

---

5 Learning more about organization
page 105

- Ask students if they know what the word *testimonial* means.
- Read the information box *Testimonials* at the top of page 105.
- Call on a student to read the examples aloud.
- Ask students if they can remember any advertising testimonials from print, Internet, television, or radio advertisements. Write some examples on the board.

1

- Read the instructions for Step 1 aloud.
- Call on students to read the headings in the chart and the examples aloud. Explain vocabulary as necessary.
- Call on a student to read the testimonial aloud.

2

- Read the instructions for Step 2 aloud.
- Have students complete the chart individually.
- Have students compare their information with a partner.

3

- Read the instructions for Step 3 aloud.
- Have students work with their partners. Encourage them to be dramatic.
- Walk around the classroom, helping students as necessary.
- Call on student pairs to share their testimonials with the class.

6 Analyzing a model page 106

1

- Read the instructions for Step 1 aloud.
- Have students read the advertisement individually.
- Call on students to read the advertisement aloud, sentence by sentence. Explain vocabulary as necessary.
- Read the instructions for 1a–b aloud.
- Have students complete 1a–b individually.

> **Answers**
>
> 1. a. Do you ever wonder how that special person in your life *really* feels about you? Now you can find out.
>   True love was hard to find before, but not anymore!
>   b. Topic sentence: The Love Meter is the quickest, easiest, and most accurate way to measure love.
>   Advertising claim: If you point it at a co-worker, friend, or romantic partner and push the "love test" button, in three seconds you will learn whether that person loves you or not.
>   Recommendation: Buy the Love Meter and take it with you the next time you meet that special person.

2

- Read the instructions for Step 2 aloud.
- Have students work with a partner.
- Go over answers as a whole class.

7 Write! page 107

1

- Read the instructions for Steps 1 and 1a–b, including the cues that follow, aloud.
- Have students complete 1a–b individually.
- Walk around the classroom, helping students as necessary.

2

- Read the instructions for Step 2 aloud.
- Have students write their advertisements (including the testimonial) on lined paper or type them. Have them skip lines. Tell students to include a drawing or photo of the customer or product. Tell them you'll collect the paragraphs after they're revised in Parts 8 and 9.

> **In your journal . . .** If time permits, read the journal entry instructions aloud. Tell students that they can also write about some favorite advertisements and their claims and recommendations. They can also write about why they like or dislike advertisements. Students can write in class or at home.

8 Editing page 108

- Read the information box *Using persuasive language* at the top of page 108.
- Call on students to read the examples aloud.
- Ask students to look back at the paragraph in Part 2, Step 1, and underline the superlatives (lightest and most comfortable).

1

- Read the instructions for Step 1 aloud.
- Have students complete 1a–f individually.
- If students are having difficulty, first have them write the superlative form of the adjectives in the box and check answers. Then have them complete the sentences.

- Have students compare answers with a partner.
- Go over answers as a whole class.

> **Answers**
> 1. a. scariest
>   b. biggest
>   c. funniest
>   d. loudest
>   e. lightest
>   f. most intelligent

2

- Read the instructions for Step 2 aloud.
- Have students who want to add superlatives revise their paragraphs from Part 7 at home.
- Have students share their revisions in groups, or have volunteers write their old and new sentences on the board.

> **Optional activity**
>
> **Superlative practice**
>
> Have students work with a partner or in small groups. Tell them to brainstorm a list of adjectives and then write their superlative forms. Compare adjective lists as a class.

9 Giving feedback page 109

Tell students that they are going to read each other's advertisements and that they will need a sheet of paper for Step 2.

1

- Read the instructions for Steps 1 and 1a–b aloud.
- Have students work in groups of three and exchange their advertisements with another group.
- Have students complete 1a–b in groups.
- Walk around the classroom, helping students as necessary.
- When they finish, ask the class, *In 1a, how many people chose (fashionable)?* See which was the most popular product description chosen. Ask how many people wrote their own ideas and what they were.

2

- Read the instructions for Steps 2 and 2a aloud.
- Have students choose an advertisement and then complete 2a individually.
- Tell students to exchange books and review their partner's answers.
- Read the instructions for 2b aloud. Then call on a student to read the example letter.
- Have students complete 2b individually.
- Walk around the classroom, helping students as necessary.
- Have students give their letters to their partner. Give them time to tell their partner the answer to the question in the letter.

3

- Read the instructions for Step 3 aloud.
- Have students revise their advertisements based on the comments they receive and other ideas they have. They can complete their revisions either in class or at home.
- Have students turn in their revised paragraphs to you.

Optional activity

Acting it out

Have students work in small groups. Have them read each member's advertisement and then choose one to act out as a short television commercial. Encourage them to be persuasive and to have fun with it. They can add to the ideas the author originally wrote if they wish. Have all the groups perform for the class.

Just for fun page 110

- Ask students if they've ever heard of a tag sale or flea market. Tell them that it is an open-air market where people sell used items. Tell students that they'll be creating a class market.
- If you wish, have students add prices to their items and pretend to sell them.

1

- Read the instructions for Step 1 aloud.
- Have students complete Step 1 individually. Make sure they are describing objects they have with them to display.
- Walk around the classroom, helping students as necessary.

2

- Read the instructions for Step 2 aloud.
- Have students complete Step 2 individually.
- Walk around the classroom, helping students as necessary.

3

- Read the instructions for Step 3 aloud.
- Call on students to read the conversation in the speech bubbles.
- Arrange the classroom for the class market. Spread items and descriptions on a few large tables, or have students push a row of desks together to serve as display tables.
- Have half of the students display their items while the other half of the class walks around the room to look at all the items and ask questions. Then have the two groups switch roles.
- Encourage students to be convincing salespeople!

12 *Lessons learned*

Overview

In this final unit, students write about an action they regret. They also learn to write a concluding paragraph.

In the prewriting activities, students practice describing situations and learn to describe the consequences of an action by adding explanations and drawing conclusions. In Part 7, students write one paragraph explaining the mistake and the damage it did and a second paragraph explaining what they learned from the experience. In the postwriting editing activity, students vary word choice by replacing common adjectives with more descriptive synonyms. In the *Just for fun* activity, students write a poem about the action they regret and make a sympathy or apology card from it.

Key points

Since students are reflecting on and assessing negative past actions, this unit has the potential to become emotional. When students share their papers, remind them not to be critical or judgmental of their classmates.

The unit combines many of the skills and techniques students have learned in previous units, such as using topic sentences, using transition words, explaining cause and effect, and writing narratives.

Useful language for this unit includes past tense verbs and adjectives to describe feelings.

Sections can be skipped. A minimal set of sections might include Parts 3, 4, 5, 6, and 7.

1 Brainstorming page 111

Ask students if they know the word *regret*. If they don't, have them work with a partner to look it up in the dictionary and share an explanation of the noun and verb with the class.

1
- Read the instructions for Step 1 aloud.
- Ask students to tell you what they see in the pictures. Provide vocabulary as necessary.
- Call on a student to read the captions under each picture aloud.

- Have students complete Step 1 individually.
- Have students compare responses with a partner.

2
- Read the instructions for Step 2 aloud.
- Have students complete Step 2 individually. Set a time limit of five minutes.
- Walk around the classroom, helping students as necessary.

3
- Read the instructions for Step 3 aloud.
- Have students compare lists with a partner and add more ideas to their own lists.
- Call on some students to read their list of ideas aloud to the class or write them on the board.

> **Later in this unit . . .** Call on a student to read this aloud.

Optional activity

Class pet peeves

Write *pet peeve* on the board. Explain to students that a pet peeve is something that another person does that bothers them a lot (e.g., being late, telling lies, or borrowing money). Give students a few minutes to write some of their pet peeves individually. Tell them not to write about specific people. Then have students stand and talk to their classmates about what three things bother them most about other people. Call on students to tell the class some of the things they learned about their classmates.

---

2 Analyzing a paragraph page 112

1
- Read the instructions for Step 1 aloud.
- Ask students to tell you what they see in the picture.
- Have students read the paragraph individually.

- Call on students to read the paragraph aloud, sentence by sentence. Explain vocabulary as necessary.
- Read the instructions for 1a–d aloud.
- Have students complete 1a–d individually.
- If your students are having difficulty, you may want to stop after lb and review.
- Ask students to raise their hands or nod at you to let you know when they have finished.

2

- Have students compare answers with a partner.
- Go over answers as a whole class. Have students write the answers to 1c–d on the board.

Answers

1. a. I learned that I should tell the truth.
   b. angry, guilty
   c. I feel bad that I told someone my friend's secret.
   d. I felt ashamed, so I said I was sorry and (I) promised never to tell her secrets again.

Talk about it. Read this aloud and have students talk with their partners for about five minutes.

---

3 Learning about organization page 113

- Read the information box *Writing an explanation* at the top of page 113.
- Call on students to read the examples.

1

- Read the instructions for Step 1 aloud.
- Have students complete 1a–d individually.

Answers

1. a. She was sad. I said I was sorry, and I'm going to take her to the movies tonight.
   b. I didn't have enough money, so I couldn't pay him back.
   c. My brother brought his friends into my room and used my computer.
   d. I promised to never lie to her again. She forgave me, but I have to work late every Friday!

2

- Have students compare answers with a partner.
- Go over answers as a whole class.

Optional activity

Judge and jury

Brainstorm a list of about five mistakes similar to the examples in Part 3 and write them on the board. Then, in small groups, have students work together to write the following: (1) what the consequences should be and (2) how the situation could be fixed. Put two groups together and have them read their ideas to each other, or have each group read their ideas to the whole class.

---

4 Working on content page 114

1

- Read the instructions for Step 1 aloud.
- Have students complete Step 1 individually. They can use an idea from their brainstorming notes in Part 1 or think of a new idea.

2

- Read the instructions for Step 2 aloud.
- Call on a student to read *The situation* and *What I did wrong* aloud. Ask students to guess how Jenny felt. Then call on a student to read *The consequences* aloud.
- Have students complete Step 2 individually. Remind students that the consequences could be their feelings, the other person's feelings, or some events.
- Walk around the classroom, helping students as necessary.

3

- Read the instructions for Step 3 aloud.
- Have students compare responses in groups of three.
- Call on some students to share their responses with the class.
- Give students time to add ideas or information to their charts.

5 Learning more about organization

page 115

Read the information box *Conclusions* at the top of page 115.

1

- Read the instructions for Step 1 aloud.
- Call on a student to read the example aloud.
- Have students complete Step 1 individually.
- Go over the answer as a whole class.

Answer

1. I should ask permission before I borrow things.

2

- Read the instructions for Step 2 aloud.
- Have students complete Step 2 with a partner.
- Go over answers as a whole class.

Answers will vary. Possible answers:

2. a. I should leave earlier.
   b. I should do my own homework. / I shouldn't let someone copy my homework.
   c. I should do what I promise to do.
   d. I should apologize in person and be more responsible.

3

- Read the instructions for Step 3 aloud.
- Have students complete Step 3 individually.
- Call on some students to share their responses with the class.

Optional activity

Stories with morals

Find two or three short stories with a moral, such as stories from *Aesop's Fables*, in the library or on the Internet and read them to the class. Read the first one with its moral to the class. Then read the second one, but don't read the moral. Have students work in groups to write their idea of what the moral is. Have groups read their ideas to the class.

6 Analyzing a model page 116

1

- Read the instructions for Step 1 aloud.
- Have students read the paragraphs individually.
- Call on students to read the paragraphs aloud, sentence by sentence. Explain vocabulary as necessary.
- Read the instructions for 1a–d aloud.
- Have students complete 1a–d individually.

Answers

1. a. I feel bad that I lost my friend Ashley's scarf. That experience taught me two things.
   b. 1, 3, 4, 2, 5
   c. bad
      guilty
      sorry
      sad
      angry
   d. I must be more careful with other people's things Ashley taught me what true friendship is.

2

- Have students compare answers with a partner.
- Go over answers as a whole class.

7 Write! page 117

1

- Read the instructions for 1a aloud.
- Call on students to read the example aloud.
- Read the instructions for 1b aloud.

2

- Read the instructions for Step 2 aloud.
- Have students write their paragraphs on lined paper or type them. Have them skip lines. Tell them you'll collect the paragraphs after they're revised in Parts 8 and 9.
- Walk around the classroom, helping students as necessary.

> **In your journal . . .** If time permits, read the journal entry instructions aloud. Tell students to try to use vocabulary and expressions from the unit. Students can write in class or at home.

8 Editing page 118

- Read the information box *Word choice* at the top of page 118.
- Call on students to read the examples aloud.
- Remind students to use a variety of vocabulary to make their writing more interesting.

1

- Read the instructions for Step 1 aloud.
- Call on a student to read the words in the box aloud. Explain vocabulary as necessary.
- Have students complete Step 1 individually.
- Have students compare answers with a partner.
- Go over answers as a whole class

> **Answers**
> 1. Good feelings: proud, excited, relieved
>   Bad feelings: angry, depressed, embarrassed, ashamed, disappointed

2

- Read the instructions for Step 2 aloud.
- Have students complete 2a–f individually.
- Have students compare answers with a partner. Encourage them to discuss differences of opinion.
- Go over answers as a whole class.

> **Answers**
> 2. a. excited, angry
>   b. relieved
>   c. depressed
>   d. disappointed
>   e. embarrassed
>   f. ashamed, proud

3

- Read the instructions for Step 3 aloud.
- Have students who want to replace any words revise their paragraphs from Part 7 at home.
- Have students share their revisions in groups, or have volunteers write their old and new sentences on the board.

9 Giving feedback page 119

Tell students that they are going to read each other's paragraphs and that they will need a sheet of paper for Step 2.

1

- Read the instructions for Steps 1 and 1a–d aloud.
- Have students exchange their paragraphs with a partner and complete 1a–d. Walk around the classroom, helping students as necessary.
- Tell students to exchange books and review their partner's answers.

2

- Read the instructions for Step 2 aloud. Then call on a student to read the example letter.
- Have students write their letters to their partner individually.
- Walk around the classroom, helping students as necessary.
- Have students give their letters to their partner. Give them time to tell their partner the answer to the question in the letter.

3

- Read the instructions for Step 3 aloud.
- Have students revise their paragraphs based on the comments they receive and other ideas they have. They can complete their revisions either in class or at home.
- Have students turn in their revised paragraphs to you.

Just for fun page 120

Bring or have students bring colored pencils or markers to class. They could also make their cards on a computer.

1

- Read the instructions for Steps 1 and 1a aloud.
- Have students complete 1a individually.
- Read the instructions for 1b aloud. Explain vocabulary as necessary.
- Call on a student to read the poem on the card aloud.
- Have students complete 1b individually.
- Walk around the classroom, helping students as necessary.

2

- Read the instructions for Steps 2 and 2a–b aloud. Point out the example in the picture.
- Have students complete 2a–b individually. If necessary, they can finish their cards at home.

3

- Read the instructions for Step 3 aloud.
- Set up a display table of all the cards or post them around the class so that all the students have a chance to see the cards.
- Encourage students to send their cards to the appropriate person. Have students report the recipient's reactions to the class.